ECONOMICS AND FINANCE

WIN-WIN GROWTH STRATEGIES

BY

Dominion Victory Judah

AN ABRIDGED DISSERTATION

Presented to the Department of

(Finance and Economics)

PROGRAM AT

Faculty of Business and Media in fulfillment of the requirements for the degree of Doctor of Philosophy in Economics and Finance

2022.

TABLE OF CONTENTS

PREFACE

We must endeavor to grow the global macro economy by pulling people out of poverty in every local economy and jurisdiction in order to have a well-represented global wealth.

It is highly imperative to note that globalization can only be genuinely effective, achieved and sustained by building strong local economies. The more local economies prosper, the more global economy would flourish.

This is common and scientific sense. The weight of an elephant cannot be borne or upheld with the legs of a chicken. It takes healthy and strong legs to uphold the weight of the entire body sustainably. Therefore it would be a mishap to think that policies that sap local economies while promoting globalization can be economically sustainable, because as local economies sink due to such policies the global economy will also crash either now or later. It has to be clear to everyone that the global economy cannot be stronger than the strength supplied from every local economy. If the economies of nations remain weak it will definitely lead to weakness and collapse of the global economy because it is natural for weak and unhealthy legs to make a person become wheelchair bound and the question is, do we want global economy to become paralyzed or bound to wheelchair?

Having said all that, I believe that we must stop politicizing economic policies and be genuine in the pursuit of economic growth in every nation, in order to create stronger, healthier and more prosperous world economy and environment for all.

Our commitment to this as leaders and individuals whether in public or private sector is a determining factor of how better the world becomes. This commitment will produce accelerated positive results in resolving the many problems and crisis that is ravaging the earth, whether economic, security, conflicts, health even governance and politics.

By conservative calculation, over 90% of world's population live either an average or below average life and these percentage of people do not actually need too much of professional terminologies and politicized environments. All they rather need is honest and effective commitment, pragmatic approach and right policies from their leaders to enable them unleash the greatness that is domiciled in them. When this is done they will definitely live happier, have ability to meet needs and have no lack. It is not too much to expect this from any government and leadership of any community globally.

There is greatness and glorious destiny in everyone you see and there are rightful things to do in order to birth or manifest such greatness but the society globally, has made many people shut down their minds in terms of positive thinking, there by disabling their capability to produce great ideas or think of greatness.

This thesis is about helping governments, leaders and nations to look in the right directions, develop and unlock the greatness and prosperity in their people, communities, economies and the world at large. Everything written here is to be seen and applied with a perspective and focus on growing local economies which will in turn boost global macro economy.

CHAPTER 1
Factors that Affect GDP Growth

Natural resources

Economic growth is the process of an economy getting larger or increasing production, usually by adding more goods and services. This is the opposite of a country's economic downturn, referred to as a recession. Natural resources, both renewable and non-renewable, and ecosystem services account for a sizeable amount of a nation's actual wealth (Chen et al., 2022). They act as the foundation upon which other forms of capital are built. They advocate for taxation, income, and the struggle against poverty. Natural resource-related sectors create jobs and frequently serve as the economic engine of underdeveloped cities. The importance of natural resources cannot be overstated. As a result, they need to be handled carefully.

Since the rate of resource extraction accelerates as the intensity of use increases, natural resources have a double-edged effect on economic growth. Natural resources are an essential part of the production process that supports economic progress. However, given the limited nature of natural resources and the need for sustainable growth, relying on their utilization, Furthermore, extensive use of natural resources thwarts sustainable growth (Pomi et al., 2021). Although the direct economic utilization of natural resources to meet human needs is relatively restricted, their economic worth to society is increased when they are converted into commodities and services.

In this case, exploiting natural resources for economic gain is crucial for long-term sustainable growth. Therefore, a balance between the provision of essential commodities and the sustainability of natural resources is an important principle for economic growth (Bilan et al., 2019). The government's crucial function is to enact laws to ensure that resources go toward long-term economic development of countries rather than just short-term revenue collecting. By developing top-notch institutions today and in the future, the so-called "resource curse" may be transformed into an opportunity.

Natural resources are this planet's "basic building blocks." They include land, water, minerals, and fossil fuels that exist in nature.

These resources form the basis for all human activities like food production and manufacturing. Natural resources may affect economic growth because they influence sustainability or environmental degradation. The first national accounts were used in the late 19th Century to calculate the size of countries' economies, but today's national accounts are much more refined.

Economic growth factors are more sophisticated than in the late 19th Century. Natural resources also play a role and can affect different industries or regions in a country's economy (Gryshova et al., 2020). The utilization of natural resources, pollution, and other environmental factors has become crucial to the prospects for sustained development and long-term economic growth. The availability of natural resources has influenced human activity and relationships between nature and civilization. Environmental issues are caused by economic activity (production, trade, and consumption). In contrast, questions about the sustainability of economic profits from the exploitation of natural resources are raised by the depletion of limited renewable and non-renewable resources.

In the 21st Century, more economic theories have been developed to assess the connection between economic growth and natural resource availability; among these are the Hicksian production function theory, balanced growth theory, and non-causality. The

Hicksian production function theory uses the economic value of natural resources to calculate the rate of return on investment (Sergi et al., 2019). It is based upon two arguments. The first argument is that using natural resources for economic purposes has a limited effect on sustainable growth; hence, it does not generate strong positive effects for future economic growth. The second argument is that technological development reduces the cost of human labor, increasing production and income from natural resources.

CONTRIBUTION TO THE RISE OF GDP

Rise of Revenue

Natural resources led to the growth of revenue, which is the result of growth in the gross domestic product (GDP). The government's primary objective is to provide the resources required for economic growth through various development plans and policies. These plans can be implemented to achieve sustainable economic growth in a country.

Natural resource management is a crucial component of economic growth since the wealth represented in natural resources accounts for a sizeable amount of the wealth of most nations, frequently exceeding the value reflected in generated capital. Due to the increase in commodity prices, several nations have witnessed a considerable increase in their natural resource earnings (Cigu et al., 2018). Non-renewable resource supplies are decreasing as a result of rising demand from countries that are expanding quickly, while harvests of renewable resources are approaching their maximum sustainable production levels. In resource-rich economies, natural resources like oil, gas, minerals, and timber are anticipated to be important. Unsurprisingly, nations with abundant natural resources can generate substantial current revenue.

Reduction of Poverty

Natural resources may be a key component of attempts to reduce poverty and generate income for nations with abundant resources. Most of the poor, especially those residing in rural areas, depend on natural resources for their livelihood. Therefore, Efforts to improve the management of natural resources can significantly and immediately lower poverty.

Creation of Employments

When creating policies for resource management, decision-makers typically have to choose between conflicting values. If creating jobs is the first aim, it could be preferable to provide many small harvesters access to quotas or harvesting rights. A strategy of most excellent sustained yield with fewer major enterprises may be desirable if increasing exports is the principal aim (Gryshova et al., 2020). This "trade-off" is common in fisheries, where fewer, larger boats may be more effective at catching fish for export, but a more extensive fleet of smaller boats may employ many people.

Adopting policies that put nations on the path to green growth may help achieve a mix of goals, including growth, employment, and long-term economic stability. Natural resources can provide a sizable amount of employment. Employment in the renewable energy industry has increased. It can continue to increase over the long term, even if employment in conventional extractive sectors has progressively decreased worldwide owing to mechanization and economies of scale.

Germany's renewable energy sector rose from 66,600 in 1998 to 259100 in 2006. A million jobs are created and provided in the renewable-related industries. According to some estimates, Germany has 1.8 million employees employed in environmental protection (Bilan et al., 2019). Sweden has an extensive and expanding environmental business. It has been there for ten years and, from 1998, employed around 1.5% of the labor force in the nation.

POLICIES TO AVOID THE "NATURAL RESOURCE CURSE"

Natural resources can be used in various ways, each with a different cost. There are options to use natural resources wisely by saving them, which means policies are required to avoid negative externalities such as over-exploitation, pollution, and environmental damage. Appropriate policies can encourage Innovation in the extraction sectors and minimize the impact of exploitation on the environment (Mačerinskienė & Aleknavičiūtė 2019). However, there is a concern that government intervention would adversely affect economic growth by causing curtailment of exploration and development activities. These policies have the effect of reducing economic and wealth growth.

Economic growth can be sustained when an appropriate intervention is undertaken in the form of the aggressive development of a sustainable ecosystem, which is possible with the right policy (Pomi et al., 2021). A sustainable ecosystem promotes growth. Policies should encourage additional economic activity and increase sectoral output to avoid the natural resources curse.

Norway's economy depends on oil reserves that account for over 16% of GDP. When the price of oil increased in 2001, Norway's economic growth rate rose to 12%. Consequently, the Norwegian economy was growing at an annual rate exceeding 10%. The Norwegian government has created a "government pension fund" where approximately one-third of all petroleum revenue is saved for future generations (Gryshova et al., 2020). Over time, the Norwegian government has accumulated more than $1 trillion in this fund. This fund helps Norway reduce capital flight, a severe problem for many resource-rich countries.

A petroleum fund helps to move Norway towards a greener economy. The additional savings from the petroleum boom are invested in renewable energy projects. This fund also helps reduce the economic volatility associated with resource-based economies, including Chile and Nigeria.

Below are examples of some policies

1. The ecological footprint of Norway - the impact of natural resource use on the environment and a sustainable economy
2. Natural Resources, Economic Development, and Green Growth in the World Economy
3. The economics of natural resources for development - ECO Economic Analysis
4. Sustainable Development: Natural Resource Based Economies: A Framework for Decision Making in Developing Countries. Rome: Food and Agriculture

Organization of the United Nations / UNEP Regional Office for Africa (FAO/UNEPROA) (2001)

5. Comparative analysis of the potential of natural resources for development - UNEP (2012)
6. A comparative analysis of resource-dependent economies and their implications for green growth - United Nations Conference on Trade and Development (UNCTAD) (2011)

A natural resource is an essential factor in every country. The Natural Capitals Approach (NCA) is a method of determining the actual value of natural resources for resource management to meaningfully contribute to a nation's economic and social development rather than just short-term growth based on unstable sources of income (Sergi et al., 2019). The NCA aims to provide stakeholders and decision makers with reliable tools to comprehend the function of renewable and non-renewable resources in an economy, improving communication, group decision-making, and logical policy for sustainable development.

Understanding the role that natural resources play in social and economic development as natural capital is essential for sustainable natural resource management and maximizing the value of natural assets. To properly value resources, it is also essential to recognize that valuation encompasses non-market values ingrained in communities and goes beyond a straightforward calculation of market prices. Resources are used most effectively for the most long-term economic value for the whole society rather than for the short-term advantage of a select few people, thanks to institutions and open, inclusive decision-making procedures.

Human Capital

Economic growth is typically associated with increasing production or consumption. These factors, however, do not paint the most accurate picture of how well an economy is performing as measured by GDP. Although GDP can be seen as a gauge for economic performance, it does not consider the quality of that growth and the sustainability of that growth. In fact, since 1990, more than 40 percent of all countries with a high growth rate have had a significant drop in their per capita income rates. The four main factors of economic growth are labor, physical capital, natural resources, and human capital (Bilan et al., 2019). Human capital consists of the knowledge and skills that a population has available to draw upon to aid in growth.

Economic growth can be attributed to the different factors surrounding human capital. The most critical component of human capital is education. Education dramatically contributes to economic growth rates. The higher an individual's education level, the more significant the contribution to an economy's income and output. Therefore, countries must invest in their workforce to ensure a high investment in human capital. Human capital, in many ways, is seen as an asset that helps economic growth.

The two-factor economic growth model is a neoclassical growth model that describes factors contributing to long-term economic growth in an economy. It can be adapted to accommodate multiple types of human capital. The conventional formulation is often used, with labor and capital as factors of production and knowledge as the third factor.

Human capital is a form of economic capital. However, unlike physical capital, it is not fixed in the amount available but rather in its development over time. Little emphasis was placed on the investment of human capital in academic literature until the 1980s when economists began to address this issue by developing empirical models based on actual data (Pomi et al., 2021). It was suggested that human capital was crucial to understanding differences in labor input which led to differences in productivity across workers.

Measuring human capital

It is measured in monetary forms as the sum of potential future earnings of the working-age population. They are using the U.K. as an example, as indicated in the figure below. The decline in the U.K. human capital indicates a rise in unemployment rates and a reduction in real wages (Marques et al., 2019). Depending on the latent earnings is a limited perspective of human capital. Earnings may not always adequately reflect all facets of human capital. The OECD takes a variety of variables into account when measuring various aspects of human capital.

Figure 1: Employed and full human capital

UK, 2004 to 2014

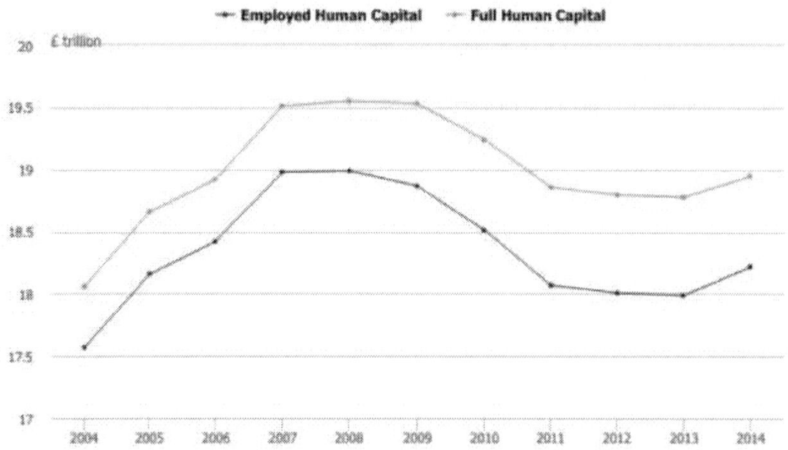

Source: Annual Population Survey (APS) - Office for National Statistics

Factors Affecting Human Capital

Skills and qualifications

The skills and qualifications a particular group of the population has also are very important as it determines their probability of employment and income (Marques et al., 2019). Many countries have implemented policies to increase their workforce's skills and qualifications.

The age structures

The age structure in a country may also affect the rate at which its economy grows. Countries with an older workforce, with a smaller proportion of young people, tend to have slower growth rates than countries with younger populations with a higher proportion of youth.

Education systems

The education systems can also affect how much growth an economy can achieve. Education systems often significantly impact the country's social and economic development (Sergi et al., 2019). Countries that provide higher education for all citizens can improve their economies by having a larger workforce with a higher level of skill and knowledge.

Work experience

Employers in most countries expect applicants to have some work experience. Experience (both positive and negative) is one factor that affects workers' productivity. Having the right skills and qualifications will lead young graduates to get work experience, which will help them secure a job and contribute more to the economy.

Emotional intelligence

Emotional intelligence is related to human capital because it is considered a form of capital (although it is not officially recognized as such). It is considered an essential factor in economic growth. It has been proposed that the importance of emotional intelligence in economic growth can be seen through its positive relationship with a country's GDP per capita, national savings rate, and the level of foreign direct investment into a country.

Social skills – communication

Social skills are also crucial for the growth and development of any country. The more developed a country's communication skills and group interactions, the more successful it can become.

Role of Human Capital in Economic Growth

Economic growth derives its primary basis from human capital. It contributes to both technical development and higher production. In actuality, the advancement rate in human capital separates industrialized and emerging nations the most. The developing nations require human capital to staff new and increasing government services, implement novel agricultural and land-use practices, create novel communication technologies, advance industrialization, and establish new educational infrastructure (Sergi et al., 2019). In his statement that "we now receive a bigger proportion of economic development from investment in men and improvements brought about by enhanced men," Prof. Galbraith is correct.

Human capital is an essential factor that all countries need to develop to ensure success in the world economy. For a country to increase its GDP, it must invest in human capital. The ability of a country to increase its GDP by investing in human capital depends on the quality and quantity of human capital available within that country. A resource-constrained economy, for example, may increase its GDP by investing more resources into educating the population (Pomi et al., 2021). In a resource-abundant economy, the same amount of resources can be used for other purposes without diminishing economic growth (Marques et al., 2019). This can be seen through the number of countries that have increased their GDP in recent years by focusing on human capital investment instead of physical capital investment.

Austria is a resource-abundant democracy and has increased its GDP from $43 billion in 2000 to $387 billion in 2014 due to its emphasis on human capital investment instead of physical capital investment within its economy (see figure 2). The United States, on the other hand, is a resource-constrained democracy that has increased its GDP from $4.8 trillion in 2000 to $16.7 trillion in 2014 due to its focus on physical capital investment over human capital investment (see figure 1).

Human capital as a factor of growth is key to an economy's productivity, significantly impacting the country's Gross Domestic Product. As the human capital of a country increases, so does its productivity. This means that a country's value of goods and services (also known as GDP) also increases with increased human capital. Therefore, GDP is positively associated with human capital, which means that growth in GDP will lead to growth in human capital investments over time.

Many researchers have shown a positive association between Human Capital Investment and GDP growth. One such example is by Hudson and McMillan (2010). At first, the researchers focused on the relationship between Human Capital Investment and GDP growth for a sample of 21 OECD countries. The researchers concluded that most countries have a positive relationship between Human Capital Investment and GDP Growth. However, statistical noise may affect some countries' findings (Sergi et al., 2019). To overcome this, Hudson and McMillan (2010) used peer-reviewed research to confirm no statistically significant difference in participation rates among the 21 OECD countries.

Importance of Human Capital

Structural unemployment

It may be difficult for people with improper human capital for modern enterprises to find employment. Today's economies face a serious challenge as a result of the rapid deindustrialization that has left many manual workers unable to thrive in a drastically changed labor market.

Quality of employment

In many countries, youth unemployment is a severe issue in the labor market. Human capital is not only crucial for the economic growth of a country. It is also essential to ensure that the jobs being created are well-paid and full-time (Prasetyo & Kistanti 2020).In many countries, most young people do not have formal education and therefore cannot lead a better life and deal with soft skills and income. This has become accepted as usual in those countries.

Economic growth and productivity

Workers with good human capital in the form of skills are more productive, leading to higher output from firms. By increasing productivity, workers also contribute to economic growth (and to economic growth as measured by GDP as well).In many countries, women and young people cannot access education and training, which hampers their ability to contribute to economic growth.

Ways of developing Human Capital

By improving the labor force's productivity, human capital can be increased. These include raising the level of notarization among working-age people and enhancing their skills, health, and education.

a) Provision of health facilities that impact the life anticipation, capability, vigor, and good health of the people
b) Provision of on-the-job training, which enhances the skill of the labor force
c) Arranging education at the primary, secondary, and higher levels
d) Study and extension programs for adults.
e) Providing sufficient migration resources to help families adapt to shifting employment possibilities.

Law

Numerous things influence economic growth. The government of a nation must uphold the rule of law and defend property and contractual rights for markets to function successfully and efficiently. All members of society must be treated equally under the law, which must be clear, accessible to the public, just, and upheld. Property ownership and use are rights that belong to both individuals and corporations. The right to education and experience are included in the notion of property, mainly since education influences income (Marques et al., 2019). The ability to negotiate with other parties using your property is part of the usage of this property. To enter into a contract, people or organizations must own the property.

As a result, contractual rights are founded on property rights and enable people to make agreements with others over the use of their property while also allowing legal remedy in the case of disobedience (Prasetyo & Kistanti 2020). If a nation's legal system preserves contractual and property rights, the World Bank deems it to have an effective legal strategy. Using a scale from 1 to 6, with one being the lowest and 6 being the best rating, the World Bank has devised a grading system for nations' legal systems based on successful protection of property rights and rule-based governance (Pomi et al., 2021). The global average rating in 2012 was 2.9. Afghanistan, the Central African Republic, and Zimbabwe had the lowest rankings of 1.5; their GDP per capita was $1,000, $800, and $600, respectively (Sergi et al., 2019). The World Bank notes that Afghanistan's weak administration, disregard for the rule of law, and low level of life have impeded its ability to expand economically.

The politically unstable and landlocked Central African Republic is a source of minors exploited in human trafficking and has inadequate economic resources. Since 1998, Zimbabwe has seen slowing development. The economy has been hampered by price restrictions and land redistribution, while the political system has been controlled by corruption and violence. Even if there has been an increase in global economic growth, those nations that lack a clear framework of property rights and an impartial legal system free from corruption have fallen far behind.

One of the most important consequences of the "law as a factor of economic growth" is the improvement of the investment environment and stable business development, thus creating conditions to accelerate economic growth.

The role of law in the development of a state depends on the kind and size of legal regulation it uses and how it uses the rule. How a state uses law significantly influences various aspects, including state administration, economic development, business environment, and international relations (Stoica et al., 2020). It is of great significance. Therefore, it is essential to investigate the law as a factor of economic growth and its effects on the economic development of a state in recent research (Prasetyo & Kistanti 2020). According to the 2012 United Nations General Assembly Meeting on the Rule of Law, "the advancement of the rule of law at the national and international levels is essential for sustained and inclusive economic growth (Pomi et al., 2021). Sustainable development, the eradication of poverty and hunger, and the full realization of all human rights and fundamental freedoms, including the right to development, all of which reinforce the rule of law."

Role of Judiciary in Economic Growth

The judiciary function is another important aspect that has to be discussed in this context. While political institutions have a significant role in shaping an economy, the court frequently resolves questions about new and impending legislation in developing nations. The judiciary is crucial in defining how new laws are applied and how to make it possible for outdated laws to be gradually removed.

The judicial system lays out how passed laws are executed and administered, while political machinery defines how the legal system of an economy is structured. However, attorneys also play a crucial role in this area in regular business (Prasetyo & Kistanti 2020). If the general counsels, senior advocates, judges, and others who carry the primary responsibility for implementing the laws are not up to par, an economy with an advanced legal system and "state of the art" legislation would nevertheless struggle to get off the ground.

The role of law in shaping an economy is essential, particularly in developing nations. Regulations play a vital role and are necessary for the development and progress of an economy. Legal institutions are critical for this purpose because they are the only devices that allocate rights between individuals and corporations. They also ensure that laws, whether in the formal or informal areas, are enforced by civil or criminal means (Sergi et al., 2019). Without these institutions, developing or progressing a country's economy would not be possible.

The judiciary plays a crucial role in shaping the economic growth of a country. The part of the court badly explains why the development of China is much higher than that of other countries with similar economic and social situations when we compare it with its neighboring states.

The more considerable significance comes from China's development adopting a unique policy and direction. It released reform enthusiasm, set up various government reform organizations, and created comprehensive laws and policies for sustainable economic growth.

The Role of Legal Norms in the Economic Development

Legal norms are a social reality formed through law-making, application, and enforcement participation. The development of legal norms is one of the typical characteristics of transformation from a traditional to modern society because these legal norms control various aspects that affect economic growth.

Legal norms are essential for economic growth and development processes. This can be understood by the mentioned matter: "Law as a factor of economic growth ."Law provides certainty. Certainty is a precondition for capital accumulation and investment, promoting economic development (Pomi et al., 2021). Since the late 1990s, China has undertaken a set of new legal reforms and increased its rate of legal growth to improve its economic competitiveness and meet its people's growing needs. The Chinese economy has increased during this period, with average annual GDP growth rates exceeding 10% in the 1990s (Sergi et al., 2019). This has been achieved while maintaining low inflation, unemployment, and a large trade surplus.

Legal norms are an essential means of managing social relationships and activities. In addition, they define the rights of individuals and organizations concerning one another and the state and its officials (Stoica et al., 2020). They include formal norms (those enacted by legal authorities) and informal norms (i.e., unwritten laws). The role of legal norms in shaping an economy is also vital, particularly in developing nations (Prasetyo & Kistanti 2020). Law is essential in this regard as it determines the rights and duties of individuals, corporations, and other bodies.

Legal reforms can significantly benefit the economy of a country. Legal reform is a suitable way to boost economic growth because it can improve government efficiency and competitiveness, increase private sector efficiency and productivity, improve corporate governance and enhance the regulatory environment. However, legal reforms could cause many problems in society too.In order to make investing certain and predictable, law is crucial. Economic development is difficult to conduct without the assurance of legal certainty because funding is scarce. The creation and administration of SEZs have not provided whole and complete legal certainty.

The legal sector has significant economic implications as a result of its close linkages to the institutional structure of trade and commerce. Financial success and the operation of commercial and institutional architecture are closely intertwined. (Chen et al., 2022).

Economic development is primarily facilitated by encouraging more sophisticated economic activity, made possible by a solid institutional framework supported by the legal community (Marques et al., 2019).Reforms. Facing the slowing of its economy, the government, in October 2006, requested help from the IMF in ways that would allow it to maintain a large trade surplus while development continues.

How does the rule of law enable economic development?

1. Protection of individual property rights- Every nation has the inalienable right to private property. The essence of personal property is that it is owned exclusively by an individual. This means that the owner can dispose of their property in any way they please and that no one can take it away from them. This is true whether this property is owned by a citizen, a corporation, or another person.
2. Universal acceptance of property rights- Property rights mean the same thing to everyone. Ideally, the creation of property rights is independent of any particular nation's history, culture, and traditions. That does not mean that no one can own property in their country as long as a just legal system protects that person's rights.
3. Protection of individual financial rights - The laws and regulations governing a nation's financial sector should be equitable. These laws should distinguish between those who can pay for the long-term investment decisions of others. In most countries, all bankruptcy laws apply to all types of debtors, not just corporations or banks.
4. Protection of individual economic rights- The economic rights of an individual include the right to sell goods and services, import goods and compete in international

markets, and hire others for these purposes (Prasetyo & Kistanti 2020). In a country where all property rights are respected, all individuals have the right to do these things.

5. Fair and equitable contract enforcement- We should be able to enter into a contract with another person and enforce it by the law. Contracts may include employment agreements, purchase agreements, and business partnerships. These contracts are necessary because they allow us to live together peacefully, help us achieve our hopes and dreams, and contribute significantly to social productivity.
6. Protections for investors- Investors need to know that their investments will be protected in some way against risks stemming from domestic instability or foreign governments that confiscate assets belonging to them.

A culture where trade and business may exist and prosper is created when citizens are adequately treated with dignity and respect. For a community to have robust, long-term economic growth, democracy is required, along with the fair and equal application of the law at every level of society and government.

"The rule of law is a crucial component of progress, not just a decorative element. It fosters an atmosphere where wealth may be developed, and the entire range of human creativity can thrive

(Pomi et al., 2021). 2008 Final Report of the U.N. Commission on Legal Empowerment of the Poor.

Entrepreneurship

Entrepreneurship has been recognized as a key contributor to long-term economic growth and development because it boosts market spending, knowledge transfers, employment, and innovation. The association between the three factors—economic growth, economic development, and entrepreneurship—has, however, rarely been scientifically quantified.

By providing cutting-edge products, services, and technology, entrepreneurs promote economic progress. Because of growing entrepreneurship rivalry, existing businesses are compelled to become more competitive. Entrepreneurs create opportunities for both long-term and short-term employment (Sergi et al., 2019). For instance, Stevenson of Harvard Business School views entrepreneurship as a type of managerial strategy rather than a specific time, such as the start-up phase of a business, or a specific person within a business, such as its founder. Stevenson defines entrepreneurship as the "pursuit of opportunity beyond resources controlled"(Marques et al., 2019). This definition fits with the focus of this article: entrepreneurship as a factor that continually stimulates economic growth and development.

New inventions tackling intractable societal issues like climate change and systemic racism are promised due to the economic, political, and social transformations brought about by entrepreneurial enterprise. Notably, the results may vary and even fail to deliver the social justice or positive development goals that were first promised. The ability to solve societal challenges has become more recognized as a critical role of entrepreneurship as it has grown more socially aware of the effects of entrepreneurial activity on such concerns (Pomi et al., 2021). Though its proponents may not be aware of it, entrepreneurs have an overall beneficial influence on economic growth, even though the research suggests that these effects vary significantly across different economic sectors. There is conflicting information regarding how successful historically relevant technologies have been at resolving the problems they address.

"Necessity" Entrepreneurship vs. "Opportunity" Entrepreneurship

Opportunity entrepreneurs, or opportunity seekers, are generally risk-takers who did not necessarily set out to become an entrepreneur. They are risk-takers who are looking for a high reward. For example:

Necessity entrepreneurs, or necessity seekers, start a business because they have no other available option for survival. Necessity entrepreneurs face circumstances that force them to be resourceful and generate income (Nepal & Paija 2019). Necessity entrepreneurs are in poverty and forced to create wealth out of thin air! Poverty breeds creativity and gives the person a reason to care. They will not typically set unrealistic goals but instead develop a plan that uses what they have. Necessity entrepreneurs tend not to concern themselves with how they will make money—they would solve a problem with no solution or at least find a way to help those less fortunate (Marques et al., 2019). Necessity entrepreneurs may know funding sources and have a broader view of their role in creating businesses.

Entrepreneurship can be defined as a learning process that involves creating, managing, and recovering from business ventures. Entrepreneurial learning opportunities exist in the places where people interact with new materials each day: work, school, family, and community.

Benefits of Entrepreneurship in the Economy

Creates and improves productivity

It has been widely held for the most of economic history that improvements to one or both of an economy's two primary building blocks, labor and capital, were the basis of economic development. It was often thought that for an economy to flourish either the labor market had to expand or capital intensity had to rise in some way.

Robert Solow, an American economist, demonstrated in 1957 that productivity gains more output per unit of input driven by innovation and account for the majority of economic development, not increases in capital or labor (Stoica et al., 2020). As businesses and workers become more productive, costs decline, earnings and incomes rise, demand rises, and economic growth and job creation accelerate up. He benefits the economy in two ways. Firstly, it stimulates new economic activity and demand, leading to growth. Secondly, it leads to Innovation and productivity improvements that lead to growth. Increases competition in the market

The existence of entrepreneurs drives up the level of competition by encouraging existing businesses to improve their products and services or lower their prices. Entrepreneurs also introduce new ideas into the marketplace, potentially improving quality and lowering prices (Marques et al., 2019). It's also important to realize that not all businesses survive. When a business fails, its resources are freed up and can be used by some other entity. This means that resources are not wasted but remain in circulation within the economy to be used by some other business. In this way, entrepreneurs contribute to economic efficiency by preventing resources from being wasted.

Reallocating efficiency is significant enough to drive macroeconomic success since ground-breaking technology advancements drive productivity. Several respected economists have pointed to the reduction in allocate efficiency in the American economy during the past two decades as the leading cause of the slowdown in productivity growth.

It creates Innovation

In addition, enterprises help the economy to grow by giving people something to spend money on. According to Kehoe (1981), the classic entrepreneurship theory is that the entrepreneur's role is to create societal value. Entrepreneurs create something new or improve upon an existing product or service to gain positive externalities and make a profit that returns to society (Cigu et al., 2018). Such positive externalities include an increase in employment opportunities, an increase in the number of goods and services provided for sale in the economy, and an increase in the overall quality of goods.

Innovation is another benefit. The more new products and services are available to consumers, the greater the demand for labor. Even if a product or service is not created by a traditional entrepreneur but by a corporate innovator, it still stimulates employment levels (though to a lesser extent than if created by an entrepreneur).

Since revolutionary technological breakthroughs fuel productivity, allocate efficiency is significant enough to generate macroeconomic success. In reality, several reputable experts have identified the slowdown in productivity growth during this time as primarily caused by the decline in allocate efficiency in the American economy over the past two decades (Nepal & Paija 2019). The growth of economies depends on ongoing Innovation, incredibly transformational or "disruptive" Innovation, and intense competition. And the efforts of entrepreneurs are crucial for these kinds of advances.

Job creation

Entrepreneurs not only create jobs for themselves, but they also create for others. Economies of scale dominated throughout the industrial age; more prominent was better, and the most significant enterprises employed the most people (Sergi et al., 2019). That started to change in the 1970s when more minor, more agile enterprises played a more significant role in the American economy due to the collapse of manufacturing and the transition to knowledge-intensive industries.

However, a few economists started questioning this way of thinking in the middle of the 1990s. By the middle of the 2000s, this idea had been wholly refuted thanks to a breakthrough in data accessibility at the U.S. Census Bureau (Stoica et al., 2020). They discovered that new and young businesses, not small ones, fuel the growth of new jobs. These researchers discovered that net employment creation's "small business impact" vanished after accounting for company age (Pomi et al., 2021). Outside of new and emerging enterprises, small businesses produce less employment than they destroy; overall, the latter effect is more pronounced.

Depending on the industry type, entrepreneurship benefits the economy by creating jobs. According to the American Psychological Association, "Innovation lays the foundation for economic growth and job creation." Jobs are created as entrepreneurs develop new industries and provide new goods and services for consumers. Entrepreneurship also creates demand for workers in other industries by increasing consumer spending.

Entrepreneurs up the level of opposition

Entrepreneurs increase competition for already-existing firms by starting new ones: lower pricing and a more comprehensive selection of products, as a consequence, benefit consumers. Researchers have established a measure of market mobility to show how new company creation affects already-existing businesses. A shift in the order of established companies according to their staff count denotes a change in market share and increased market mobility (Mačerinskienė & Aleknavičiūtė 2019). This effect is most pronounced when taking into account entrepreneurial activities five years previous to the start-up, suggesting that start-ups have a significant time lag before they impact market mobility (Stoica et al., 2020). Furthermore, creating new businesses encourages existing businesses to perform better, indirectly increasing competition.

FACTORS THAT LEAD TO THE GROWTH OF THE ECONOMY BY ENTREPRENEURS

Motivation

Businesses are kept alert and motivated to strive continually to grow and adapt if entrepreneurs are regularly supported in both good and poor economic times. Even if some individual businesses fail, entrepreneurs provide the vitality that keeps economies strong and thriving (Cigu et al., 2018). All economies, including capitalist ones, support entrepreneurship. Entrepreneurship is starting to be supported and encouraged in managed economies like China. They have learned that entrepreneurial endeavors, formerly seen as a challenge to the status quo, are essential for preserving economic competitiveness and attaining long-term success.

Creation of policies

The laws governing property rights and government policies significantly impact a nation's capacity for Innovation. While safeguarding intellectual property rights encourages entrepreneurship and Innovation, maintaining material property rights assures that any money created remains in the hands of the businessman.

In many economies, bureaucratic barriers limit operations that are motivated by Innovation. Because entrepreneurs may operate flexibly and adapt their business venture to changes in the market, deregulated economies with freely running markets and effective licensing will have more prospects for entrepreneurship (Mačerinskienė & Aleknavičiūtė 2019). The fair and uniform application of rules and regulations is also crucial.

Administrative obstacles for new businesses should be minimal, including the time it takes to register, the number of stages involved, and the number of rules, taxes, and reporting requirements (Gryshova et al., 2020). Leading nations that support business enable organizations to register for a business within a day without requiring routine renewal. This may be done by establishing a cutting-edge online e-administration for all joint enterprises.

Entrepreneurship is among the backbone of the economy. It plays a significant role in economic growth. Governments will support and maintain their entrepreneurs and even draw in innovators from other nations if regulatory barriers are lowered and corruption is eradicated (Sergi et al., 2019). Therefore, by modifying the regulatory environment in favor of entrepreneurship, the policy may most effectively affect the level of entrepreneurial activity.

Technology

Governments or enterprises can shape this factor. Governments can help shape the economy by restricting firms or providing incentives. Technology is one of these areas where government policy and the private sector can influence growth in an economy (Nepal & Paija 2019). Technology has been and continues to be a significant driver of economic growth in advanced economies as it helps entrepreneurs compete in global markets and raises productivity levels. Technology is one of the most critical factors in economic growth.

Economists have often struggled to explain why some countries have experienced long periods of superior growth relative to others. Endogenous growth theory, which argues that technology is the driving force behind economic growth, emerged due to this failure (Pomi et al., 2021). It is also important to note that while technology is a critical factor in economic growth, other factors such as investment are also vital.

Theories that explain Technology as a factor in Economic Growth

Solow-Swan Model Theory

One theory is the Solow-Swan model, which is based on the growth of productivity based on the accumulation of technology and capital. As a result, this increased productivity is correlated to higher wages. This theory does not include a theory of human capital, structural change, or international trade (Stoica et al., 2020). The Solow-Swan model assumes the economy is at full employment with constant returns to scale in production and no technological change.

The new growth theory is also based on the Solow-Swan model; however, it is more complex. It explains why countries do not grow at a constant rate but instead experience accelerating growth spurts that are not necessarily tied to increases in capital and labor. This theory argues that "exogenous" sources can sustain technological change and that the accumulation of physical capital is not the only source of growth. Consequently, this model describes the convergence process in per-capita income across countries. Although the new growth theory explains the technological change in human capital, international trade and structural change are still not included. New sources of growth such as technological adaptation, increases in physical capital, and social organization are also included.

Another theory is Robert Solow's neoclassical growth model. It is based on the concept that increasing technology positively affects economic growth and production. The neoclassical theory holds that the more employed people, the higher output becomes (Gryshova et al., 2020). This theory cannot explain why some countries experience faster growth; however, this theory is still valuable for economists as it can be used in empirical work.

This theory focuses on the Solow-Swan model's four factors: consumption, investment, population growth, and capital accumulation. The neoclassical theory applies to policymakers because it provides them with statistical tools. It can be used to examine whether technology has a positive or negative effect on economic growth and can also be used to forecast future periods of growth.

The factor that determines technological change is Innovation in human capital; thus, this is essential in shaping economic growth. Many examples of technological change have shaped economic growth in the past (Sergi et al., 2019). For example, the automobile was a significant factor in 20th-century economic growth as it was essential in shaping urban areas and providing affordable transportation. Technology is also crucial in economic growth as it increases efficiency within traditional sectors and new developments, particularly within emerging technologies and industries. Finally, technological change has been more recent and occurs at a faster pace today. Changes in technology can be measured by higher levels of research and development spending, among others.

Schumpeterian Theory

In general, the idea of Schumpeterian theory is based on the development of new production processes. This theory holds that economic growth is based on Innovation, allowing new products to enter the market. J.A. Schumpeter believed that technological change is essential in shaping economic growth and aiding innovations; this theory is also known as "creative destruction." This is because new technology allows for the creation of more efficient businesses (Mačerinskienė & Aleknavičiūtė 2019). For example, e-commerce has allowed businesses to expand their markets and reach consumers in other countries (Nepal & Paija 2019).

Furthermore, Schumpeterian theory holds that innovations generate more profits for firms and investors. These profitability gains provide resources for future innovations. In this way, technological change can boost economic growth as it allows for further Innovation and expansion of the economy. For example, the smartphone has become a must-have for many workers and consumers.

Endogenous Growth Theory

The endogenous growth theory is based on the idea that a company's ability to innovate and increase its productivity is based on the level of an endowment from a particular resource. Endogenous market growth is given by "G," where "G" is a constant that describes the rate of growth and "k" describes the size of the investment necessary to make new technologies. The theory states that this endogenous growth can be used to forecast future periods of economic growth (Cigu et al., 2018). For example, if "G" decreases, the growth rate will be lower, and there will be less investment in new technologies. The Solow-Swan model is based on the concept that total factor productivity is the driving force behind economic growth. This model holds four production factors: labor, capital, natural resources, and technology. Increased technology allows for higher production output, eventually increasing wages. More specifically, this model assumes constant returns to scale in production and that the economy is at full employment with no technological change. The Solow-Swan model can be separated into two parts: labor and capital (Sergi et al., 2019). However, it is only valid for analyzing economic growth. The Solow-Swan model does not examine technological change, structural changes, or international trade. Consequently, this model does not explain why some countries grow faster than others.

An evolutionary-institutional theory of economic growth

Technology is a crucial factor in economic growth and development. However, technological change has not always been the primary or sole factor that drives economic growth. Over the past two centuries, economists have concluded that human capital is essential in determining an economy's ability to adapt and innovate. This is mainly due to increasing population size, which indicates increasing human capital. The evolutionary-institutional theory of economic growth holds that an increase in human capital allows for more technological advances and subsequent productivity increases (Gryshova et al., 2020). This theory is based on the idea that human capital can be increased by education and training with access to better technology. Additionally, this theory holds that Innovation and technological change are influenced by legal institutions, access to financial markets, and government regulation. Last, this theory argues that technological progress combines evolutionary processes, including incremental and radical disruptive innovations.

The evolutionary-institutional theory of economic growth identifies four factors critical to technological change and economic growth: institutions, capital, human capital, and knowledge. Institutions are the rules that govern the market. For example, regulations protect consumers and investors. Institutions include property rights, contract enforcement, and information sharing systems (Mačerinskienė & Aleknavičiūtė 2019). Capital is crucial in technological change as it allows firms to invest in Innovation. Capital comes from different sources and includes deposits from people who save money in banks or investors who buy stocks or corporate bonds. Capital allows firms to invest in productivity-enhancing technologies and growth (Nepal & Paija 2019). Human capital is essential in economic growth as it provides a workforce with excellent skills and knowledge. Human capital includes education, training, and learning from observation. Knowledge is the most critical factor in technological change as it can be used to invent new products, processes, and services (Bilan et al., 2019). Knowledge is based on trial-and-error development and accumulated wisdom throughout history. Technology provides the opportunity for knowledge to be utilized for further discovery, ultimately becoming technological change.

Factors that connect technology to economic theory

1. Learning, both from the past and from others

To develop new technologies, we must look back to what has already been done and other technologies that have successfully solved a problem. The scientific method allows us to compare different solutions based on their efficiency, cost-effectiveness, and ease of use. Understanding which knowledge is most important allows companies to make more effective future research and development decisions. Consequently, learning-by-experience and technological diffusion allow technologies to spread faster and more efficiently.

2. Capital.

Capital is the money invested in a product or service's research, development, production, and marketing. Many economists argue that capital allows firms and governments to fund research and development into new technologies. This R&D allows companies to discover innovations that can increase productivity, reducing consumer costs (Sergi et al., 2019). Furthermore, this R&D establishes new industries and creates jobs, providing a positive externality for the economy.

3. Knowledge.

This factor deals with the ability of companies to continuously develop new technologies and adapt to changes in their industry. To create new products, one must learn from the mistakes of others or take innovative approaches to solve problems. To efficiently innovate, companies need access to data that shows how consumers prefer certain products (Cigu et al., 2018). Accessing data from various forms of market observation allows firms to adapt their processes and improve existing technologies.

4. Human capital. Human capital includes the knowledge, skills, and abilities of an individual or firm. Knowledge is information that has been acquired through education or observation. Skills are physical abilities that allow humans to perform tasks faster than if they did not have skills at all. Human capital also includes experience with various tasks and acquired knowledge and skills needed in specific jobs or industries. In general, if an organization possesses sufficient human capital, it becomes more efficient despite the competition from other firms. This is because human capital is a "collective good," as the economist Ronald Coase explains.

5. Institutional factors.

Institutions are rules and regulations that shape how an economy operates. The main goal of institutions is to maximize social welfare and achieve Pareto efficiency (the allocation of resources that results in an equitable distribution of benefits and burdens) for society. Two leading institutions are government policies and laws and market-determined incentives or norms (Sergi et al., 2019). Government policies and laws affect technological change by impacting the motivation of corporations to undertake Innovation. Market-determined incentives and norms affect technological change by influencing the behavior of individuals in their day-to-day lives. These two types of institutions work together to influence technological change.

Population

The population influences economic growth. A country with a large population will have a higher GDP because it has more working people and the potential for more opportunities. However, if the population increases too much, it may overcrowd the country, leading to lower quality of life. For example, if a country has a population of 5 million and has the potential for high economic growth (Nepal & Paija 2019). If the population increases by 2 million in the next 20 years, there might be overcrowding in significant cities and lower quality of life.

On the other hand, a country with a large enough technical force could harness the larger workforce to produce higher economic growth more effectively. In this case, a country could have a population of 10 million with the potential for growth and quality of life. This influence of population is not always apparent. For example, China (population 1.3 billion) and Kenya (population 37 million) have different growth rates, even though there are only 16 times more people in China. Contracting the population can lead to declining economic growth. If the population shrinks too much, the country could underperform in terms of GDP and other products. For example, Japan's population is contracting, and its GDP has declined.

Capital

The population is not the only factor that affects economic growth. A country's level of available capital also affects its ability to produce goods and services. If a country has only a small amount of capital compared to its population, it will not be able to produce as many products as other countries (Bilan et al., 2019). However, if a country has more capital, it can produce as many products as they want. For example, suppose a country has average capital of

$100 billion and an average population of 1.3 billion. In that case, it will be able to produce goods and services with an average level of output compared to other countries (Mačerinskienė & Aleknavičiūtė 2019). Another factor that influences the amount of capital available is the quality of investments. For example, the quality of investments has been declining in Japan because Japan is not used to making investments according to international standards.

Factors that connect population to economic growth

1. Education

Another important factor that connects population to economic growth is education. If people in a country are not educated, they will not be able to contribute their full potential to the country. If there is high unemployment in a country, it could be due to a large number of uneducated workers. If a country has a large population of educated people, they will be able to get better jobs and higher salaries. This is what occurred in India after they made many educational reforms. Another factor related to education is the country's technology level. If the country does not have enough technology, it will be hard for people to become highly productive and work at a higher capacity.

2. Public health

Another factor that connects population to economic growth is public health. If people in a country are healthy, they can work effectively. They will not have to pay the cost of health care. Also, they will be able to work more and produce more goods and services per person. This is because a healthy population can produce more goods and services in a shorter period (Nepal & Paija 2019). For example, If a country has a population of 100 million people with 1/3 having high levels of cancer and diabetes, then the GDP would be reduced by $200 billion because they would have to spend money on sanitation, medicines, and other expenses related to treating these illnesses (Chen et al., 2022). However, if the population is healthy, there would be no extra expenses related to health, and the GDP would be higher.

3. Infrastructure

Another important factor that connects population to economic growth is infrastructure. A country with a high-quality infrastructure will have lower production costs. This will lead to higher levels of economic growth. For example, if there are many potholes and bridges in a city, it would take longer to travel around the city, which would cause an increase in the cost of transportation (Mačerinskienė & Aleknavičiūtė 2019). The additional cost will be passed on to companies which would degrade the economy as companies raise prices based on increased operational expenditures. On the other hand, if there were high-quality roads and bridges, transportation would be more accessible. This would lead to lower costs of production, which could increase the level of economic growth.

4. Technology

Technology is also an essential factor that connects the population to economic growth. When technology is not efficient, the amount of goods produced is limited. However, when technology improves, the number of products per person increases. For example, suppose a country has technology that makes it hard to produce goods because the machinery requires many people to run it, and there are not enough workers. In that case, production will be lower because there are not enough workers (Nepal & Paija 2019). However, if a country has technology that allows more people to work and produce more goods, then the country's economy will grow at a faster rate. For example, if a country had a population of 100 million people and developed technology that allowed for more goods to be produced per person. There would be an increase in the country's GDP (Sergi et al., 2019).On the other hand, if a country had technology that made it hard for people to produce goods because there were not enough workers available or there were not enough production methods, then economic growth would be lower.

5. Taxation

Taxation is one more factor that connects population to economic growth. If a country has a large population that contributes to the GDP, but there are levels of income inequality, the population will have lower expenditure on consumption per capita. For example, if the population is large and contributes $500 billion to the GDP, but there are high levels of income inequality. Only a tiny percentage of people would be contributing economically. If the population were higher and had a low level of income inequality, then more people would be contributing to the economy.

Using this reasoning, taxation can also influence economic growth. High taxation in a country where a large amount of money from the government comes in will impact the country's ability to grow (Cigu et al., 2018). If the country has high taxation and a large population, people will have less money to spend on consumption. However, if the country has low taxation and a large population, more people will be able to spend money on consumption.

6. Capital accumulation

Capital accumulation is also another factor that connects population to economic growth. If a country has resources but little capital, it can be challenging for citizens to access those resources. For example, if a country only has $1 billion of capital, it will make it hard for citizens to get the resources they need to produce goods and services. As a result, citizens will have fewer options of what to buy (Mačerinskienė & Aleknavičiūtė 2019). This can reduce the country's potential for growth because citizens will have less money to spend on consumption.

Additionally, if a country uses capital efficiently, it will increase the number of goods and services produced. For example, if a country had $1 billion of capital but put $1 billion into an investment-based economy where they only make 10% interest on their investments, then people would not be able to produce any goods and services. As a result, the country would have to increase its capital to produce more goods and services per person.

Capital accumulation is crucial because it connects the population to economic growth. If a country has a large population and little capital, then there will be fewer people working and producing goods. As a result, the GDP will decline. On the other hand, if there is high capital, more people will work and produce more goods, which can cause economic growth.

7. Population demographics

A large country will have a more significant potential for economic growth if it has a growing and healthy population. A larger, young population will be able to enter the workforce faster than an old population while still producing goods and services. Additionally, the amount of money a country can support would be higher with a larger population. If a population grows, it will have a higher population-to-GDP ratio because the GDP can be divided by the number of people to get the GDP per capita (Chen et al., 2022). If the population is not growing or declining, then GDP per capita and the GDP will be lower because there are fewer people.

When comparing the United States' economic growth with other countries, one must remember that the U.S.'s economic growth outpaced all other industrialized countries in that same era due mainly to its formative role during World War I and II. The United States economy also benefited from much higher capital levels, which was achieved partly through foreign investment and the U.S.'s geographic isolation from the main theaters of war (Sergi et al., 2019). Additionally, most European countries were heavily damaged or entirely devastated by the war, resulting in a lower potential for growth.

Another comparison to be made is between the economies of Japan and South Korea. Both countries experienced similar population growth and demographic change during their respective periods of high economic growth (Mačerinskienė & Aleknavičiūtė, 2019). The two countries differed, however, in the degree to which their economic growth was fueled by industrialization and modernization. While South Korea's economic growth occurred primarily through industrialization, Japan experienced a much more significant portion of its growth through modernization.

Infrastructure

Infrastructure includes the roads, railways, ports, airports, electric grid, and water supply necessary for goods transport and distribution on a national scale. They also include schools where people receive training for professions vital to growing economies. In this paper, only the infrastructure necessary for trade is considered.

The infrastructure consists of two parts; the first is called "hard" infrastructure, which refers to the physical structures like roads and railways. The second one is called "soft" infrastructure, which includes institutions like market regulations and education systems. It also depends on achieving important national goals (Cigu et al., 2018). To link supply chains and efficiently transport products and services across borders, the economy needs a solid infrastructure. Infrastructure connects metropolitan families to opportunities for higher-quality employment, healthcare, and education. The usage of sustainable energy and public transportation reduces greenhouse gas emissions. Broadband networks, water supply systems, and the generation and distribution of energy are all subject to the same economic principles.

Infrastructure does not directly affect economic growth, but it does have an indirect effect. If a nation is deficient in complex infrastructure, it will be difficult for a firm to transport its goods to the market. This implies that firms are less likely to invest in less-developed counties.

Starting from the 19th Century, economists have observed that countries with good quality infrastructure but lower income levels show higher economic growth rates than their socio-economic equal with poor infrastructure (Nepal & Paija 2019). In other words, a positive correlation exists between growth rates and infrastructure quality. The larger this correlation is, the more critical infrastructure is for economic growth.

Infrastructure can be a beneficial factor for businesses, but it also has several constraints. One of the major problems encountered by firms that want to invest in an underdeveloped country is political risks.

The fact that a local government will not allow them to build means that they will not be able to develop their business as they planned. Another problem is the low quality of education. This means that the quantity or skill level of the local workforce is too low to provide a good return on investment (Mačerinskienė & Aleknavičiūtė 2019). Finally, governments can be reluctant to finance firms in underdeveloped countries. Therefore, better options exist in other parts of the world with better infrastructure and educated workers.

Economic expansion and infrastructure are mutually dependent. First, infrastructure encourages economic growth, and second, infrastructure improvements result from economic growth. Infrastructure is vital to economic growth as firms must transport their products to the market (Chen et al., 2022). Infrastructure construction takes place in the context of an economy's overall supply chain, and several factors influence the decision-making process. First, a cost-benefit analysis considers the costs of building infrastructure such as power and roads compared with current returns from operating businesses in that area.

Factors that lead to the connection of infrastructure and economic growth

a) The direct productive sectors, such as agriculture, industry, and transportation, employ the output of infrastructural sectors like power, water, and transportation as inputs for production (Sergi et al., 2019). Since the former's availability is insufficient, the latter's asset usage is insufficient.

b) The expansion of infrastructure, such as transportation, considerably boosts productivity.

c) Infrastructure is key to modern technology in almost every industry.

d) Numerous studies have found a strong correlation between infrastructure development and GDP growth. According to this research, a 1% increase in infrastructure stock corresponds to a 1% increase in per capita GDP.

e) Studies have also shown that infrastructure services in low-income nations typically provide 6.5% of the overall value added. This percentage rises to 9% and 11% in middle-income and high-income nations, respectively.

Infrastructure should be sustainable, resilient, and inclusive, with the most influence on boosting economic recovery in the near term and long-term stability. This kind of transformational infrastructure can contribute to achieving universal prosperity. Transformative infrastructure delivers long-term prosperity for future generations, enduring social and economic benefits for everybody, and the circumstances for the shift to a resource-efficient, sustainable economy (Cigu et al., 2018). It is adaptable to take on new trends and problems as they arise, take advantage of technology advancements, and include better solutions as they become available. Since transformative infrastructure is more durable and robust than traditional infrastructure, it can respond to crises more effectively and accrue more significant advantages over time.

Importance of Infrastructure

Infrastructure Facilitates Production

Both social and economic infrastructure facilitates production. The presence of high-quality infrastructure ensures production and productivity increases. Infrastructure simplifies transferring commodities and raw materials, reducing inefficiencies, leading to practical resource usage, and eliminating waste.

Investment is encouraged by Infrastructure

Infrastructure creates an atmosphere that encourages investment. Facilities shortages deter investment. For instance, if there is no fundamental infrastructure like transportation and communication, an investor won't invest.

Infrastructure Creates Production Connections

Through both forward and backward linkages, infrastructure fosters economic growth. In other words, infrastructure creates opportunities for one industry to grow due to the growth of another through forward and backward connections. With the availability of adequate infrastructural facilities, economic expansion transforms into a dynamic process (Gryshova et al., 2020). A forward connection will aid in explaining this. For instance, if irrigation facilities enhance agricultural output, allied companies that rely on agriculture for raw material supply will also see a rise in output.

Market Size is expanded by Infrastructure

Infrastructure increases market size. A producer can distribute his goods globally and even internationally thanks to the quick and economical transfer of raw materials and finished items in quantity.

Reduction of poverty

The economy would benefit from better management of the economic infrastructure in terms of output, revenue, and employment. Additionally, it will directly benefit the poor, hence lowering poverty. Lower manufacturing costs of DPAs and increased supply elasticity of items should have an anti-inflationary impact.

Infrastructure is vital to growth and development. However, it is also essential that infrastructure be created in a way that lasts a long time and can be modified to accommodate future growth (Chen et al., 2022). Each country has its own infrastructure needs, and they do not need the same infrastructure that other countries need. The best way to provide this is through planning, design, and implementation based on local factors such as the culture and history of the country.

Infrastructure and Economic Growth

Infrastructure is the backbone of economic growth. By providing access to people's desired benefits, such as power and reliable transportation, the infrastructure helps improve productivity, leading to higher wages and higher standards of living.

Infrastructure and Productivity

The rate of return on investment in infrastructure increases with the level of productivity improvement. The more significant the difference between actual and potential output and productivity, the higher the rate of return on investment in infrastructure.

Infrastructure and Competitiveness

Infrastructure is the key to competitiveness. Infrastructure generates the factors of production, such as land, labor, capital, and materials, which allows businesses to produce goods and services that others cannot (Cigu et al., 2018). By making a country more competitive, the economy will grow faster.

Infrastructure and Poverty Reduction

Investments can reduce poverty in infrastructure. Investments in infrastructure allow people to improve their health through better roads and electricity, build homes, and live in a safe environment.

REFERENCES

Bilan, Y., Mishchuk, H., Samoliuk, N., & Grishnova, O. (2019). ICT and economic growth: Links and possibilities of engaging. Intellectual Economics, 13(1), 93-104.

Chen, H., Tackie, E. A., Ahakwa, I., Musah, M., Salakpi, A., Alfred, M., & Atingabili, S. (2022). Does energy consumption, economic growth, urbanization, and population growth influence carbon emissions in the BRICS? Evidence from panel models robust to cross-sectional dependence and slope heterogeneity. Environmental Science and Pollution Research, 29(25), 37598-37616.

Cigu, E., Agheorghiesei, D. T., Gavriluță, A. F., & Toader, E. (2018). Transport infrastructure development, public performance and long-run economic growth: a case study for the Eu-28 countries. Sustainability, 11(1), 67.

Gryshova, I., Kyzym, M., Khaustova, V., Korneev, V., & Kramarev, H. (2020). Assessment of the industrial structure and its influence on sustainable economic development and quality of life of the population of different world countries. Sustainability, 12(5), 2072.

Mačerinskienė, I., & Aleknavičiūtė, R. (2019). National intellectual capital influence on economic growth in the European Union countries.

Marques, A., Martins, I. S., Kastner, T., Plutzar, C., Theurl, M. C., Eisenmenger, N.... & Pereira, H. M. (2019). Increasing impacts of land use on biodiversity and carbon sequestration driven by population and economic growth. Nature ecology & evolution, 3(4), 628-637.

Nepal, R., & Paija, N. (2019). Energy security, electricity, population and economic growth: The case of a developing South Asian resource-rich economy. Energy policy, 132, 771-781.

Pomi, S. S., Sarkar, S. M., & Dhar, B. K. (2021). Human or physical capital, which influences sustainable economic growth most? A study on Bangladesh. Canadian Journal of Business and Information Studies, 3(5), 101-108.

Prasetyo, P. E., & Kistanti, N. R. (2020). Human capital, institutional economics and entrepreneurship as a driver for quality & sustainable economic growth. Entrepreneurship and Sustainability Issues, 7(4), 2575.

Sergi, B. S., Popkova, E. G., Bogoviz, A. V., & Ragulina, J. V. (2019). Entrepreneurship and economic growth: the experience of developed and developing countries. In Entrepreneurship and Development in the 21st Century. Emerald publishing limited.

Stoica, O., Roman, A., & Rusu, V. D. (2020). The nexus between entrepreneurship and economic growth: A comparative analysis on groups of countries. Sustainability, 12(3), 1186.

Toader, E., Firtescu, B. N., Roman, A., & Anton, S. G. (2018). Impact of information and communication technology infrastructure on economic growth: An empirical assessment for the E.U. countries. Sustainability, 10(10), 3750.

Tsaurai, K., & Ndou, A. (2019). Infrastructure, human capital development and economic growth in transitional countries. Comparative Economic Research. Central and Eastern Europe, 22(1), 33-52.

Unnikrishnan, N., & Kattookaran, T. P. (2020). Impact of public and private infrastructure investment on economic growth: Evidence from India. Journal of Infrastructure Development, 12(2), 119-138.

Urbano, D., Aparicio, S., & Audretsch, D. (2019). Twenty-five years of research on institutions, entrepreneurship, and economic growth: what has been learned? Small Business Economics, 53(1), 21-49.

Zhou, G. (2018). The Influence of China's Population Aging on Economic Growth. In International Conference on Economics, Finance, Business, and Development.

Zulham, T., Dawood, T. C., Farlian, T., Saputra, J. U. M. A. D. I. L., Juliansyah, R. O. L. L. I. S., & Hadi, F. A. J. R. I. (2021). The Nexus of Human Development Index, Economic and Population Growth On Environmental Degradation In Aceh Province

, Indonesia. WSEAS Trans. Environ. Dev, 17, 314-320.

CHAPTER 2
Sovereign Wealth Funds (SWF) and Foreign Exchange Reserves (FER)

This book will first analyze by definition and history of both Sovereign Wealth and foreign exchange reserves. The foreign exchange reserve will summarize the history of the gold era, the 1997 financial crisis, and after the 2008 financial crisis.

The article also outlines the contribution of Sovereign Wealth Funds (SWF) and Foreign Exchange Reserves (FER) to the economies. Several factors help the two to stabilize the economy. FDIs are suitable for the economy. Using Sovereign wealth funds and Foreign Exchange Reserves to attract foreign investors will enable them to contribute to economic growth. In this paper, we are analyzing how SWFs and FERs attract FDIs. The last part of this article will analyze why nations need to adopt the two.

Sovereign Wealth Fund

Megginson & Fotak (2016) claimed that global asset owners that are both significant and varied continue to be sovereign wealth funds (SWFs). They are the host governments' free budgetary resources that are invested following various mandates. A Sovereign Wealth Fund is a type of investment fund that collects money from investors and invests in multiple assets to earn returns (Gilson & Milhaupt, 2017).

According to the US Treasury, SWFs are government investment entities backed by foreign currency assets and run independently of official reserves. The IMF likewise characterizes SWFs as state-owned investment companies financed by foreign currency assets, but it further distinguishes the SWFs according to their objectives (Bahoo et al., 2020).

1) The 1950s saw the creation of the first funds. For a nation with a budget surplus, sovereign wealth funds were created. The Kuwait Investment Authority, founded in 1953 to invest extra oil earnings, was the first sovereign wealth fund. Kiribati established a fund to retain its revenue reserves just two years later. Up until the creation of three significant funds, no new activity happened (Megginson & Gao, 2020).

The size and quantity of sovereign wealth funds have grown significantly during the past few decades. The SWF Institute reports that 98 sovereign wealth funds (SWF) are operational in 2021, coming from 70 different nations and having completed 450 operations—an increase of 171% from 2020 (Bykanova et al., 2017).

Mohaddes & Raissi (2017) explained that SWFs are defined into two, Commodity Versus Non-Commodity Sovereign Wealth Funds. The difference between the two funds is how they are financed. Commodity Exporting goods helps to support sovereign wealth funds. Nations that export a product will experience higher surpluses when its price rises. In contrast, a deficit is generated when the price of that commodity declines, which might harm an export-driven economy. By making investments in several sectors, a sovereign wealth fund serves as a stabilizer to diversify the nation's finances. Usually, extra foreign currency reserves from current account surpluses are used to finance non-commodity funds (Mohaddes & Raissi, 2017).

SWFs are beneficial to the population and the economy of a nation. SWF may get funds from several sources according to Amar et al. (2018). Popular sources include trade surpluses, bank reserves that may build up due to budgetary excesses, foreign exchange operations, proceeds from privatizations, and government transfer payments. SWF may get funds from several sources. Popular sources include trade surpluses, bank reserves that may build up due to budgetary excesses, foreign exchange operations, proceeds from privatizations, and government transfer payments. Real estate and private equity account for more than half of SWF alternatives allocation, with SWFs controlling over 16% of the world's assets under management (AUM) in the latter sector (Garg & Shukla, 2021).

The sovereign wealth Fund has two primary functions, namely, 1) To ensure that there is the stabilization of the economy through diversification and 2) To provide future generations with wealth. The development of international investing depends heavily on the emergence of SWFs. According to the 2022 statistics on SWFs, Norway has the largest SWFs (Al Ayoubi & Enjolras, 2022).

Foreign Exchange Reserve

Tong & Wei (2021) claimed that Foreign Exchange Reserve is the amount of liquid and readily-available foreign currencies held by their respective central banks. Banknotes, deposits, treasury bills, and other government securities are FERs. The above assets have several purposes, but the most important is to provide backup funds for the central government agency if the national currency becomes insolvent or devalues faster than expected. It is usually a common tradition in countries globally to hold significant reserves in their foreign exchange in the World Bank.

A central bank's capacity to buy local currency with reserves assets is a liability to the central bank (Golder et al., 2022). Central bank executes monetary system policy, the number of foreign exchange reserves can alter accordingly. Still, this impulsive should be studied broadly in the circumstance of the degree of capital quality, the exchange rate authorities, and other components. Trilemma, or the impossible trinity, refers to this situation. As a result, in an idealized world where capital flows freely, a nation with a fixed exchange proportion would not be able to implement its monetary policy.

Foreign exchange reserves started before the Asian Fiscal crisis of 1997. Before the crisis, the exchange of gold prices (Arslan & Cantú, 2019).

However, US dollar served as a modesty currency under the Bretton Woods system, making it a component of a country's official worldwide reserve assets. From 1944 until 1968, the US dollar could be exchanged for gold direct the Federal Reserve System. In1968, only central banks were permitted to do so, and after 1973, no individuals or organizations were allowed to do so. No significant currency has been converted into gold using government gold reserves since 1973. Individuals and institutions purchased gold in the private industry just like other products (Lien et al., 2018).

After 1997, countries in Southeast and East Asia started building up their foreign exchange reserves significantly because their levels were to be too low and prone to market credit booms and crashes. This buildup has significant effects on the developed world economy today since it forced out investment and caused the developed world economy to virtually come to a crawl, giving rise to the current negative interest rates (Lien et al., 2018). When a new financial crisis hit the world in 2007, the US Federal Reserve set up central bank liquidity swaps with other institutions. Authorities in developed nations pursued fiscal and monetary policies that were too expansionary, which caused several emerging market currencies to appreciate. Policies seeking to stop capital inflows and further reserve buildup are to implement in response to opposition to appreciation and concern about lost competitiveness, according to Adhikari (2018).

A frustrated Brazilian official referred to this trend as a currency war. Again in 2016, following the commodities crash, Mexico had warned China of the possibility of starting a currency war. With 3.46 trillion USD in reserves and foreign currency liquidity in 2022, China has by far the highest global reserves of any country on the planet (Pinshi, 2020). As China's internal economy continues to improve, foreign investment there is increasing rapidly, providing a substantial assurance for foreign exchange reserves.

According to Boz et al., foreign currency is deposited into local banks by exporters in the country (2020). Business people are paid in dollars, euros, or other prevalence by their business partners. Merchandise then convert them into local currency. They use it to compensate their neighborhood vendors and workers. The difficulty of this strategy has increased as global trade has become more straightforward and currencies have become more complicated. A country's economy might suffer grave consequences if its foreign exchange reserves were to run out. Even if the country has significant gold reserves or abundant natural resources, those assets lack the liquidity of foreign exchange reserves. The incapacity of a government to promptly spend and purchase products might undermine public trust in the currency and cause broader market instability (Golder et al., 2020).

The US dollar remains the most common currency held by central banks (62.25%), followed by the Euro (20.26%). Japanese yen and British pound sterling make up roughly 5% of total holdings. In contrast, the Australian dollar, Canadian dollar, and renminbi of the People's Republic of China each makeup less than 2%.

Although gold and silver can make up a sizeable portion of reserve assets in some situations. There was an omission of gold prices in the IMF figures (Adhikari, 2018).

The world's reserves total $7.48 trillion, and they are held by emerging and developing nations. With more than $3 trillion in reserves, the PRC is in the first place, followed by Japan.

Sources: IMF Statistics

Contribution to Stabilization of Economy

Together, SWFs and FERs help to stabilize the economy through financial markets hedging against global risks. They also help to stabilize financial needs by providing liquidity during times of heightened uncertainty. This can be proven because SWFs and FERs hold large sums of capital that can be moved into or out of financial markets when needed (Singh, 2019).

They enable the countries during the crisis:

In 2008 during the global financial crisis, SWFs and Foreign exchange played a significant role in enabling nations to recover from the situation. A study done by Lane& Milesi-Ferretti (2018) explained that SWFs gained notoriety by assisting the banks in developing economies when the capital flows had halted. Central banks took their time using monetary policy rolls to help the financial firms.

Foreign exchange Reserves act as a backup plan for a country during a crisis. Another example is the economic and political situation in Sri Lanka in 2022. According to Visual Capitalist, the nation stopped making its debt payments in May and now owes its creditors $51 billion. Due to an increasing inability to pay for imported fuel, food, and medicine, inflation is currently at about 40% according to Bhowmick (2022). According to estimates, foreign exchange reserves have decreased by 99%, from $7.6 billion in 2019 to just $50 million.

The international economy almost reached a complete standstill during the COVID-19 epidemic, and monetary policy alone did not provide a solution. Governments used broad fiscal measures in a way that had not been seen since the conclusion of World War II. The fiscal ability of those nations with sovereign wealth funds allowed them to expand expenditures, deal with emergencies, and cut taxes when necessary to boost their economic system.

Table 2: SWF Direct Investments by Value ($Billion)

According to Nnamocha et al. (2017), FERs makes the dollar a haven during a crisis. Nations use foreign exchange reserves to maintain a stable exchange rate, exports priced competitively, crisis liquidity, and market confidence. The dollar is particularly alluring because it work as the world's reserve currency and is utilized frequently in commercial transactions abroad. The most significant gold reserves in the world serve as additional security. Compared to the major competing currencies, the so-called "Greenback" reached its most crucial level in twenty years. Due to indications that the US Federal Reserve would raise interest rates more quickly than anticipated, investors have started pouring money into it claimed to Lin (2020).

Nations used four primary strategies with sovereign wealth funds during the pandemic:

1. Using stabilization and saving money for expenditure by governments.
2. Strategic resources actively supporting pandemic relief initiatives
3. Strategic financing supporting domestic goals notwithstanding COVID-19.
4. Strategic and opportunistic hybrid investments made using savings assets in global marketplaces.

They stabilize financial markets:

The financial system is crucial to the market. It enables the financial intermediation mechanism, which facilitates the movement of funds between savers and borrowers and guarantees that funds are spent efficiently to support economic expansion and development. Since foreign exchange reserves are maintained in financial assets of some type, usually short-term government bonds denominated in hard currencies, they offer current yields and experience swings in value as a result of changes in interest rates and exchange rates (Farrar & Ariff, 2017).

Many economists say that an SWF can act as a stabilizer in the financial markets. If a country has to leave its currency and external debts, it can avoid serious consequences from a state of default by enacting sovereign wealth funds. These funds need to know their buying power in the national currency after the new system is established and how much these reserves would appreciate over time (Meng, 2020).

SWFs also help to stabilize financial markets. In this way, sovereigns can use SWFs to bring down the cost of capital for companies. First, as SWFs are long-term capitalist with no immediate calls on their possession and hold primarily leveraged holdings, they are better equipped to ride out market downturns or even buck tendencies, according to Roll (2019).

This offers preliminary proof that SWFs could lessen market volatility. Additionally, SWFs have lately boosted local equities markets and financial institutions in various nations, notably in the Middle East (Amar et al., 2018). Second, to reduce the negative price consequences of their transaction, major SWFs may undertake portfolio re-allocations gradually. Third, as long-run investors who modify the global capitalist base, SWFs might boost market efficiency, reduce volatility, and expand market depth.

This helps in stabilizing the economy by making other items such as shares and bonds more stable. When SWF was first introduced, it helped create a stabilization fund that helped countries become stable. However, some countries may use their foreign exchange reserves to make loans in global financial markets; how long they can do this is unclear. In short, SWFs help to stabilize financial markets according to Aizenman, J (2020).

It is helpful to think about how a growing accumulation of assets in SWFs may alter the pattern of global capital flows to assess SWFs' impact on global financial markets. In reality, nations having significant "excess reserves," or reserves above their typical balance of payments needs, may choose to allocate these assets among their portfolios in a way that prioritizes return above liquidity. Therefore, a juxtaposition of traditional reserve portfolios versus those based on market capitalization can show where future capital flows will come from (Aizenman, 2020).

They can act as a counter-cyclical fiscal policy instrument:

Meng (2020) Fiscal policy actions that offset the impacts of the economic cycle are known as counter-cyclical fiscal policies. "When the economy is sluggish, for instance, counter-cyclical fiscal policy moves can include raising expenditure on the government or lowering taxes to encourage economic recovery.

Both foreign exchange reserves and sovereign wealth funds have a significant role in stabilizing and boosting the output of their economies." SWFs may boost output by stabilizing markets. However, the reserves of a country's central bank can also be used as a counter-cyclical fiscal policy instrument to stabilize and boost the output of their economies when there is a recession (Taguchi & Ganbayar, 2022).

The Reserve bears the danger of starting inflationary pressures if it tries to accelerate economic development by increasing the money supply for an extended period. As a result, it will eventually have to deal with the possibility of balancing these forces. Most economists concur that inflation over time is essentially a monetary issue. Statistics show that nations with relatively slow money growth rates have relatively slow inflation rates (Carlino et al., 2020).

They help countries to avoid the reach of capital controls:

Capital controls are a policy that restricts the investment and movement of funds within and out of a country. In reality, they may be used to evade restrictions on capital movements (Li, 2017). Capital controls inhibit the free flow of funds within and from an economy. Capital controls have been applied to protect national security and limit exchange rate fluctuations.

In this case, the use of foreign exchange reserves by central banks helps to avoid the reach of capital controls. The SWFs can help countries without critical shortages of funds to prevent a government from imposing capital controls (Farrar & Ariff, 2017).

They reduce the risk that markets may experience in developing countries:

There is an agreement in international relations that countries should develop their economies sustainably and avoid taking on too much financial or otherwise debt (Ossowski, 2021).

How do Sovereign Wealth Funds (SWF) and Foreign Exchange Reserves attract FDIs? The two financial tools, SWFs and foreign exchange reserves are designed to remove the uncertainty in investing in these areas. Foreign exchange reserves, or SWFs, are generally large, liquid, and stable assets. These assets help FDIs reduce risk and make long-term investments that help enhance enterprises' productivity, efficiency, and competitiveness.

Moreover, these assets also help strengthen the national balance sheet (Farrar & Ariff, 2017). In addition, foreign exchange reserves and SWFs act as insurance for financial assets, so if a firm is bankrupt, there would be an exit option for FDIs. The majority of the countries operate under the rule of law. Moreover, many countries have an adequate legal framework governing bankruptcy and insolvency procedures.

Moreover, experts also claim that SWFs help attract FDIs because they help boost productivity. There are a few reasons to explain this phenomenon. Firstly, the high investment rate provided by SWFs helps boost capital accumulation and productivity. Secondly, SWFs also help to provide a more flexible exchange rate. It, therefore, provides a safety net for firms by easing financial volatility (Kamiński, 2017).

The SWF attracts FDIs by providing a haven for investors in a risk-free environment. This means that the fund's investment decisions are based on commercial criteria and not political pressure, thus generating more economic benefits than the fund provides. Their investments in other countries help improve their infrastructure and develop their economy. This is particularly beneficial for poorer nations that may not be able to afford certain services, such as education and health. This causes a ripple effect and generates more growth (Reddy, 2019).

Foreign exchange reserves boost confidence in FDIs and strengthen their investment. By making FDIs confident in the fund's ability to repay debts, they have an option to reduce the risk of investing in countries that have low credit ratings. They also improve the overall financial stability and smooth capital flows by making bad debts more manageable if they do happen to occur. Therefore, SWFs help restore confidence in global financial markets and provide a safe environment for FDIs (Farrar & Ariff, 2017).

SWFs also help make foreign investors believe in the economy; among the popular investment strategies that SWFs use is investing in equities and bonds to earn higher returns. In this way, SWFs attract many foreign investors to invest in these countries. SWFs may also help boost confidence among domestic and foreign investors because they can help stabilize national economies. For example, SWFs can protect against unstable exchange rates, which in turn helps to stabilize the economy.

Foreign exchange reserves help to enhance confidence, as they are a safety net for private investors and the government. The government can also use SWFs to stabilize markets and keep the value of currencies up. SWFs help to enhance confidence because they make private investors believe in the economy, which will lead them to invest (Farrar & Ariff, 2017).

Why Nations need to adopt Sovereign Wealth Funds (SWF) and Foreign Exchange Reserves (FER).

Stabilizing the economy

The most crucial reason nations need to adopt Sovereign Wealth Funds (SWF) and Foreign Exchange Reserves (FER) is that they help stabilize economies. As the economy increases, the SWFs will move in tandem with those changes, reducing market volatility. Through this process, SWFs and FERs reduce economic uncertainty, which enables nations to attract Foreign Direct Investments (FDIs) (Akacem et al., 2020). However, the world economy is not perfect. There will always be some nations that do not have sovereign wealth funds, and there will also be a few nations that accumulate too many foreign exchange reserves.

During the global financial crisis of 2008–2009, the lack of SWFs or FERs caused a liquidity freeze in some countries that did not have these mechanisms in place (Okafor et al., 2021). While this challenge may have been overcome in nations with SWFs and FERs, it would have likely become an economic disaster if SWFs and FERs were not in place. SWFs are government-owned investment funds that oversee national assets, such as oil or other mineral resources, real estate holdings, infrastructure, or agricultural property. Governments often set up sovereign wealth funds to manage their nations' extra cash.

To help stabilize the currency markets:

The other reason nations need to adopt SWFs and FERs is that they help stabilize currency markets. As the economy grows, many countries accumulate a lot of foreign exchange reserves. The massive holdings of foreign reserves lower the value of their currencies, meaning that nations with too much money can manipulate their markets by selling off their accounts (Akacem et al., 2020). That causes unstable currency markets and weak economies. On the other hand, as the economy goes down or shrinks in some nations, there is not enough money to buy back all of its currency on the international market (Ramady, 2021). This can lead to substantial drops in national currencies. When currency markets are weak, it causes problems for nations because many of their imports will become too expensive and discourage economies from developing (Akacem et al., 2020). In response to this problem, many nations have started to establish sovereign wealth funds under their governments, which can also help stabilize currency markets by managing the trade balance of nations.

To encourage foreign investment in the local economy and infrastructure:

This reason is closely related to the previous one. Foreign investment will help a nation to develop. As economies grow, nations need investments to help provide jobs for their citizens. It can help boost and stabilize an economy and attract FDIs from other countries. It is a well-known fact that capital inflows (both direct and portfolio) lead to economic growth (Okafor et al., 2021). A nation's capital inflows will provide a country's economy with funds to invest in new or existing businesses that can help boost all sectors of national economies (Singh, 2019). As FDIs return their investment to the home country, it will create jobs and economic growth for the entire population. This benefit can boost a nation's economy, providing extra jobs and money for the government to use in other sectors of their economies. Nations with SWFs and FERs attract more FDIs, giving the government more money to help improve the economy (Ramady, 2021). Since the government has funding, it can implement policies encouraging businesses to invest in other sectors of the economy.

To help the economy adapt smoothly to economic changes:

As the economy grows and develops, nations need to keep up with technological changes. To do so, they will need to attract FDIs from other nations or countries worldwide. Sovereign wealth and foreign exchange reserves help a nation adapt to new technological changes by providing them with the needed funding for their infrastructure projects, which will help them grow and compete effectively in markets (Akacem et al., 2020). As this happens, new jobs that were not available will also be generated. Most nations prefer to hold their "excess" revenues in foreign assets (Singh, 2019). They do this because they want their money to grow faster than it would at home and do not want it to be vulnerable to inflation. The only problem is that this extra money attracts speculative investment, leading to bubbles, financial instability, and currency volatility (Okafor et al., 2021). Foreign Exchange Reserves (FERs) help prevent a significant shift in the economy by stabilizing currency values on the international market.

To help avoid future economic crises:

The 2008-2009 global financial crises were one of the primary reasons governments began to focus on SWFs and FERs. Minor downturns in specific sectors of the economy could potentially cause their entire countries' economies to fall apart. This can cause massive job losses and social instability, leading to a downward spiral for many years. Nations need to build up their foreign exchange reserves to help their economies grow during hard times and avoid recession or depression. Through FERs, a nation can manage the economy and infrastructure to help it avoid any economic crises. The first reason is that foreign exchange reserves act as an insurance policy for nations. If a nation faces a global economic crisis, it can regain stability by using its foreign exchange reserves to buy back its currency in exchange for other currencies (Okafor et al., 2021). The second reason is that when a nation's economy goes down, the currency of the nation will become weak in the international market. Most tend to hold their "excess" money in foreign banks and corporations overseas to prevent this from happening.

To eliminate the risk of short-term foreign debt affecting the economy:

Today's significant problem many nations face is that their currencies are too weak in the international market. Their economies are not growing fast enough, and they cannot borrow money in the long term to invest in their infrastructure (Akacem et al., 2020). This can cause a nation's economy to decline or shrink and make it much more difficult for these nations to attract FDIs from other countries. The solution to this problem is to build up foreign exchange reserves to ensure that a nation's currency stays strong enough in the market so FDIs will want to come and invest (Singh, 2019). This will help the nation's economy to grow and develop. Another key reason to build up foreign exchange reserves is that as nations accumulate more foreign currency, it becomes less volatile (Okafor et al., 2021). When a nation's currency is too weak in the international market, it can lead to unstable and weak economies. By having FERs and accumulating them over time, a nation will be able to stabilize its economy (Ramady, 2021). This can help prevent future economic crises from happening.

CONCLUSION

Due to the similarities of both tools, sovereign wealth funds and foreign exchange reserves can help stabilize a country's economy by lowering risks associated with economic change. Both have similar goals, which include attracting FDIs, providing growth capital to existing companies, providing credit to new companies, and helping economies remain stable (Braunstein, 2017).

Foreign exchange reserves are more liquid, while sovereign wealth funds can be more diversified and have a longer-term horizon. Both SWFs and foreign exchange reserves can attract FDIs, but foreign exchange reserves may be considered a safer option for investors. At the same time, SWFs may offer more long-term growth opportunities for investors. The stability of SWFs results from the institutional structure (Lavelle, 2017).

REFERENCES SWF/FX RESERVES

Megginson, W. L., & Fotak, V. (2016). Rise of the fiduciary state: A survey of sovereign wealth fund research. A Collection of Reviews on Savings and Wealth Accumulation, 163-212.

Gilson, R. J., & Milhaupt, C. J. (2017). Sovereign wealth funds and corporate governance: A minimalist response to the new mercantilism. In Corporate Governance (pp. 463-487). Gower.

Akacem, M., Miller, D. D., & Faulkner, J. L. (2020). Oil, Institutions, and Sustainability in MENA. Springer Books.

Okafor, C., Madu, C., Ajaero, C., Ibekwe, J., Bebenimibo, H., & Nzekwe, C. (2021). Moving beyond fossil fuel in an oil-exporting and emerging economy: Paradigm shift. AIMS Energy, 9(2), 379-413.

Onah, V. C., Ihegboro, I. M., & Ojiakor, I. External Reserves and Economic Growth in Nigeria.

Ramady, M. A. (2021). Financial Regulation and Liberation: Saudi Arabia's Path towards True Global Partnership. Springer Nature.

Singh, A. K. (2019). India-West Asia Economic Relations; The Role of Sovereign Funds (Doctoral dissertation, Jamia Millia Islamia New Delhi).

Bahoo, S., Alon, I., & Paltrinieri, A. (2020). Sovereign wealth funds: Past, present and future. International Review of Financial Analysis, 67, 101418.

Megginson, W. L., & Gao, X. (2020). The state of research on sovereign wealth funds. Global Finance Journal, 44, 100466.

Bykanova, O. A., Akhmadeev, R. G., Kosov, M. E., Ponkratov, V. V., Osipov, V. S., & Ragulina, Y. V. (2017). Assessment of the economic potential of sovereign wealth funds. Journal of Applied Economic Sciences, 12(1), 70-84.

Mohaddes, K., & Raissi, M. (2017). Do sovereign wealth funds dampen the negative effects of commodity price volatility?. Journal of Commodity Markets, 8, 18-27.

Amar, J., Lecourt, C., & Kinon, V. (2018). Is the emergence of new sovereign wealth funds a fashion phenomenon?. Review of World Economics, 154(4), 835-873.

Garg, R., & Shukla, A. (2021). Sovereign wealth funds: A critical analysis. Business Analyst, 41(2), 25-47.

Al Ayoubi, K., & Enjolras, G. (2022). Does disinvestment from fossil fuels reduce the financial performance of responsible sovereign wealth funds?. Journal of Multinational Financial Management, 100731.

Arslan, Y., & Cantú, C. (2019). The size of foreign exchange reserves. BIS Paper, (104a).

Lien, D., Lee, G., Yang, L., & Zhang, Y. (2018). Volatility spillovers among the US and Asian stock markets: A comparison between the periods of Asian currency crisis and subprime credit crisis. The North American Journal of Economics and Finance, 46, 187-201.

Tong, H., & Wei, S. J. (2021). Endogenous corporate leverage response to a safer macro environment: The case of foreign exchange reserve accumulation. Journal of International Economics, 132, 103499.

Golder, U., Islam, M. N., & Kayser, M. S. (2020). Impact of foreign exchange reserve, exchange rate and crude oil price on Dhaka stock exchange index: An empirical evidence from vector error correction model. Indian Journal of Finance and Banking, 4(1), 134-143.

Adhikari, D. (2018). Impact of exchange rate on trade deficit and foreign exchange reserve in Nepal: An empirical analysis. NRB Economic Review, 30(1), 36-48.

Pinshi, C. (2020). Dollarization and Foreign Exchange Reserve: Debate on the Effectiveness of Monetary Policy in DR. Congo.

Boz, E., Casas, C., Georgiadis, G., Gopinath, G., Le Mezo, H., Mehl, A., & Nguyen, T. (2020). Patterns in invoicing currency in global trade.

Singh, A. K. (2019). India-West Asia Economic Relations; The Role of Sovereign Funds (Doctoral dissertation, Jamia Millia Islamia New Delhi).

Lane, P. R., & Milesi-Ferretti, G. M. (2018). The external wealth of nations revisited: international financial integration in the aftermath of the global financial crisis. IMF Economic Review, 66(1), 189-222.

Song, L., & Zhou, Y. (2020). The COVID-19 pandemic and its impact on the global economy: what does it take to turn crisis into opportunity?. China & World Economy, 28(4), 1-25.

Bhowmick, S. (2022). Understanding the Economic Issues in Sri Lanka's Current Debacle. ORF Occasional Paper,(357).

Bortolotti, B., & Fotak, V. (2020). Sovereign wealth funds and the COVID-19 shock: Economic and financial resilience in resource-rich countries. BAFFI CAREFIN Centre Research Paper, (2020-147).

Nawo, L., & Njangang, H. (2022). The effect of covid-19 outbreak on foreign direct investment: do sovereign wealth funds matter? Transnational Corporations Review, 14(1), 1-17.

Nnamocha, P. N., Obioma, A. P. B. K., Igwemma, A. P. A. A., & Nwoko, I. A. (2017). Foreign Exchange and Industrial Sector Growth in Nigeria (1981. Foreign Exchange, 8(24).

Lin, M. H. (2020). China upside down: currency, society, and ideologies, 1808–1856. BRILL.

Farrar, J., & Ariff, M. (2017). Sovereign wealth funds and foreign exchange reserves as state wealth. In Islamic Wealth Management. Edward Elgar Publishing.

Meng, C. (2020). Sovereign Wealth Funds as International Institutional Investors 1: A re-evaluation. In The Routledge Handbook of State-Owned Enterprises (pp. 372-389). Routledge.

Roll, S. (2019). A sovereign wealth fund for the Prince: Economic reforms and power consolidation in Saudi Arabia (No. 8/2019). SWP Research Paper.

Amar, J., Lecourt, C., & Kinon, V. (2018). Is the emergence of new sovereign wealth funds a fashion phenomenon?. Review of World Economics, 154(4), 835-873.

Aizenman, J. (2020). Macroeconomic challenges and the resilience of emerging market economies in the 21st century.

Taguchi, H., & Ganbayar, J. (2022). Natural Resource Funds: Their Objectives and Effectiveness. Sustainability, 14(17), 10986.

Carlino, G., Drautzburg, T., Inman, R., & Zarra, N. (2020). Partisanship and Fiscal Policy in Federal Unions: Evidence from US States.

Li, J. (2017). Investment terms and level of control of China's Sovereign Wealth Fund in its portfolio firms. The Oxford Handbook of Sovereign Wealth Funds, 367.

Farrar, J., & Ariff, M. (2017). Sovereign wealth funds and foreign exchange reserves as state wealth. In Islamic Wealth Management. Edward Elgar Publishing.

Ossowski, R. (2021). Sovereign Wealth Funds in Resource-Rich Caribbean Countries. Editors, 241.

Reddy, K. S. (2019). Pot the ball? Sovereign wealth funds' outward FDI in times of global financial market turbulence: A yield institutions-based view. Central Bank Review, 19(4), 129-139.

Kamiński, T. (2017). Sovereign Wealth Fund investments in Europe as an instrument of Chinese energy policy. Energy Policy, 101, 733-739.

Blonigen, B. A. (2019). Foreign direct investment (Vol. 72). World Scientific Publishing Company Pte Limited.

Braunstein, J. (2017). The domestic drivers of state finance institutions: evidence from sovereign wealth funds. Review of International Political Economy, 24(6), 980-1003.

Lavelle, K. C. (2017). Sovereign wealth funds and foreign policy. The Oxford Handbook of Sovereign Wealth Funds, 182-207.

CHAPTER 3 Impact of RMB on Chinese foreign exchange and economic growth

From 1989 to 2014, China's economy and currency system grew at an annual pace of 9.1%. This expansion has drawn the attention of policymakers and experts throughout the world (Kwan, 2018). The lower RMB exchange rates are seen to have boosted China's economy while hurting the economies of its trading partners. After over 38 percent appreciation since 1994, the Renminbi (RMB) still does not fulfill the expectations of trading partners. The sluggish rate of RMB appreciation has been criticized by the international community (Enderwick, 2018). Increasingly, the US government is urging China to adjust its currency strategy since the RMB was overvalued versus the US dollar (USD) by 40% according to the US Congress in 2007 (Zhang and Zhang, 2018). Because the RMB exchange rate appears to have had a significant role in stimulating the Chinese economy, trading partners are becoming increasingly concerned.

The Chinese government is working to raise the value of the RMB so that it may be traded more freely on the international currency market (Jin et al., 2022). Because of this, the primary goals of our study are to examine the long- and short-term dynamics of the RMB real exchange rate and economic growth, to examine the structural changes brought about by the 2005 currency policy reform, and to examine the effects of global financial crisis on the RMB exchange rate in 2008. Real exchange rate (RER) fluctuations and economic development have previously been linked (Wang and Jiang, 2019). Undervalued currencies, according to this theory, aid GDP growth, whereas overvalued currencies harm it. Trade partners are increasing pressure on the RMB to appreciate because they feel that China's economy is being fueled by the currency's low value. Despite the RMB's continued rise, Chinese authorities must respond to these challenges by making necessary modifications to the currency policy. It is the goal of this research to dispel a fallacy about the RMB exchange rate system and examine the link between RER and economic development (Mo, 2018). An overview of the Chinese economy and currency policies will be offered before the conversation begins.

In the last two decades, there have been two major changes in the value of the Chinese yuan. In 1994, the Chinese government implemented a single monetary system. In 2005, the single fixed currency policy was abolished and the managed floating exchange rate system was adopted. China has a big quantity of foreign reserves in order to maintain a stable currency (Qian et al., 2022). Since 2005, it has grown at an exponential rate, reaching a record in 2012 of $3,311 billion. There has been an increase in both GDP and the Consumer Price Index (CPI). The average yearly growth rate was over 9%, but the political crisis in 1989 led to a significant decline. Since the introduction of the market economy in 1992, it has been largely steady (Xing, 2019). The CPI curve, on the other hand, exhibits more ambiguity. The price mechanism change was responsible for the sudden rise and fall that occurred around 1994. China, on the other hand, has seen an unexpected rise in its exports. Since China joined the World Trade Organization (WTO) in 2001, trade volume has expanded significantly, but the 2008 global financial crisis had a substantial impact. When it comes to global trade, China has been the world's top exporter and importer since 2009. China's FDI in the lower (Umar and Sun, 2018). Prior to 1990, there was little foreign investment. From 1978 to 1984, FDI totaled $4.1 billion. Foreign investors began to flock to China in 1992 when the market-oriented economy was implemented and the open door policy was pushed to its limits. The growth of China is intertwined with the regime of regulated floating currency rates, to trading partners (Dieppe et al., 2018). As a result, they are bursting at the seams with queries aimed at uncovering China's development secret.

Research Objectives

The main aim of the study is to determine the impact of RMB on Chinese foreign exchange and economic growth. The study will also discuss on the link between the Real exchange rate and economic growth.

Literature review

Modern foreign trade is far more intricate and influential. It is linked to economic growth and the stability of the currency. The result of a volatile currency, overseas commerce and the local economy are frequently affected. The section will review the studies on the impacts of RMB on Chinese foreign exchange and economic growth.

Foreign exchange

Since the early 1980s, researchers have become more interested in the link between the stock market and the foreign currency market. Due to a wide range of nation selection and measuring methodologies, there are still a lot of discrepancies in the findings made thus far. Data from the U.S. stock market from 1974 to 1978 was subjected to a simple regression analysis by Zucker-Marques and da Silva (2022), who found a high positive correlation between monthly share price and effective exchange rate data in the US. Looking at the monthly share prices of American multinational corporations and the USD exchange rates between 1980 and 1986, a substantial negative association between currency exchange rates and share prices. According to Wang et al. (2021), discovered a modest link between exchange rate changes and stock market prices after repeated regressions using exchange rate, interest rate, inflation expectation, and securities price.

There is a correlation between the strength of a country's economy and its currency's influence on share prices. Currency depreciation, for example, was detrimental to the economic growth of nations that rely heavily on imports. It was, on the other hand, favorable for export-oriented countries (Cheng et al., 2018). In spite of the existence of Granger causality between the exchange rate and the stock price, Chey and Hsu (2020), discovered that there was no long-term equilibrium between the two variables. Qin et al. (2018), used daily data from 1/3/1986 to

14/11/1997 to run Granger causality tests on seven nations affected by the Asian financial crisis. Granger causality was shown to exist in South Korea, the Philippines, Indonesia, and Malaysia, but not in Japan and Thailand, according to the findings of the study. Exchange rates and stock prices, on the other hand, did not show any evidence of Granger causation in Singapore. From 1994 to 2000, Kwan (2018) used monthly stock market and exchange rate data from Pakistan, India, Sri Lanka, and Bangladesh to perform empirical study. In Pakistan and India, long-term and short-term stock markets had little effect on the exchange rate. Bidirectional Granger causation between the stock market and exchange rate could be demonstrated in the other two nations. Interest rates and the value of the dollar were the most significant economic and financial factors affecting the stock price of a corporation. Pacheco Pardo et al. (2019), revealed through empirical study that exchange rate variations had a substantial impact on local enterprises as well as import and export companies' cash flow.

Domestic foreign exchange

Until 2005, China's RMB exchange rate was based only on the US dollar and used a single set exchange rate mechanism. Because of this, the window of opportunity to investigate the link between China's exchange rates and stock prices is limited (Das, 2019). The following is a synopsis of the relevant research: the stock market in China had just a tiny effect on the currency rate and no evident relationship between the two (Sun and Park, 2021). Because China's exchange rate, capital account, and rational procedures for stock price creation had not yet reached marketization, this situation occurred in large part as a result. According to McDowell (2019), China's stock market was positively and negatively impacted by the appreciation of the yuan, which was evaluated from a theoretical standpoint. China's stock market's globalization may be accelerated by an appreciation of the yuan, which might lead to an increase in stock market prices. One of the primary drawbacks of the renminbi's appreciation was that it might potentially disrupt the financial sector and limit the independence of the monetary policy.

The empirical research, Ito and McCauley (2020), found that the stock share index had a negative correlation to RMB/USD exchange rate appreciation, with the stock price rising along with it. Duarte and da Silva (2022), used daily data from the average RMB/USD exchange rate and the Shanghai Composite Index closing price to test for a co-integration link. In the long term, the two variables were found to be in balance with one another. The VAR and VEC models were used to assess Granger causality. Consistent with previous findings, the Granger correlation between exchange rates and the stock price is one-way. Using daily data from July 22, 2005 to October 31, 2008, Shaikh et al. (2021), The SSE Composite Index and the midpoint price of the Yuan versus the USD were used as indicators of the currency's exchange rate. An exogenous variable was included to the vector autoregressive model to represent the Chinese-American differential distributed throughout the sample interval. Only in 2006 was there a long-term equilibrium link between the two variables (Xu, 2022).

There was no long-term equilibrium between the two variables in 2005, 2007 and 2008. In their study, Iqbal et al. (2020) concentrated on economics. This global financial crisis made extensive use of two key metrics: RMB exchange rate and Shanghai Composite Index. Various lag periods were used to see whether the Granger causality maintains. Two-variable Granger causality was identified by researchers. Using a one-year NDF of the Yuan against the USD and the SSE Composite Index as indicators, Maggiori et al. (2019) created a vector autoregressive model and performed a co-integration test. The long-term equilibrium between the two variables was discovered. And Chiang (2022), who studied the data from April 30, 2010 to March 31, 2014, also looked at it. Using the exchange rate and share price as indicators, it was discovered that there was a long-term equilibrium relationship between these two variables. In addition, the degree of effect of stock prices on the exchange rate was more apparent.

The RMB exchange rates

Many academics and policymakers have been intrigued by China's statement in 2005 that it will transition to a controlled floating exchange rate regime. De facto, despite claims to the contrary, the RMB exchange rate is still tied to the US dollar in relation to a basket of various currencies (Jia et al., 2021). However, scholars are still debating whether the RMB policy adjustment in 2005 had any structural consequences. Despite the fact that some studies have discovered structural impacts, others have concluded that no structural fractures occur (Zhang et al., 2022). Changes in Chinese currency policy have clearly benefited the country's economy. According to Sun et al. (2019), shows that China's current economic development is driven by the export of labor-intensive items. This might lead to China overtaking the United States as the world's largest economy by 2015. Factor accumulation, rather than productivity increase, is at least in part responsible for this rise. Though China's currency system has been criticized by the international world, the managed floating exchange rate policy has been crucial to the regional economy because it paves the way for monetary cooperation and regional currency stability in East Asia (Ji et al., 2019).

There is a short-term appreciation of the RMB from the inflow of financial money, and a long-term appreciation of the RMB from a rise in the labor force. However, (Qin et al., 2018) find that the RMB exchange rate fluctuates within a small band around the equilibrium level. In other words, the RMB is not always undervalued. Trade, population, liquidity constraints, and government investment are all factors that affect the equilibrium exchange rate of the RMB (Ma and Wang, 2019). Research on the relationship between exchange rates and growth often focuses on how the existing exchange rate regime affects growth as well as how exchange rate volatility affects growth.

Impact of exchange rate regime on economic growth

Differing exchange rate regimes have been studied to see if they have different effects on economic growth in the past. An increasing amount of evidence shows that a flexible exchange rate system is preferable than a fixed exchange rate regime for growth (Zhang and Zhang, 2018). The growth of emerging economies is favorably connected with an intermediate exchange rate system; however, this regime is less flexible. Compared to fixed exchange rate regimes, sophisticated economies demonstrate no major influence. For industrial nations, Guzman et al. (2018), show that different classifications of exchange rate regimes provide comparable findings. Flexible exchange rate policies tend to lead to better growth rates in these countries. The announcement of a peg to the US dollar and the currency rate's de facto stability usually has favorable impacts on development in developing nations and emerging economies. The growth of a country's economy may be hampered if the currency is exclusively linked to the USD. Dollarization has a negative impact on growth if the degree of dollarization is greater (Ibrahim and Alagidede, 2018). Even in rising economies, the choice of exchange rate regime has minimal effect on long-term growth.

The linkages between Real exchange rate and economic growth

Real exchange rate undervaluation and economic growth have been proven to be positively linked in prior research, although this connection should be substantially greater in developing nations (Lengnoo and Masih, 2018). Growth can be negatively or positively affected by changes in the RER's equilibrium level. Exchange rate misalignment, ambiguity, and disequilibrium are some of the terminology used to characterize RER fluctuations by (Barguellil et al., 2018). Defining exchange rate misalignment is a matter of measuring the RER's divergence from equilibrium. Economic growth is negatively impacted when the exchange rate is very erratic, while growth is positively impacted when the exchange rate is moderately volatile (Aloui et al., 2018). Realistically, emerging-market currencies tend to be either undervalued or overpriced. If the currency's exchange rate is lower than it should be or if it has depreciated considerably, the currency is undervalued. A currency's worth is overestimated when the exchange rate is overvalued (Simtowe and Yi, 2018). An inflated exchange rate inhibits economic growth, whereas an undervalued exchange rate boosts it (Vasani et al., 2019). However, there are divergent perspectives among Huong (2019), on the impact of a low exchange rate on the various components of GDP. Undervalued currencies in emerging nations have no negative impact on exports, but they do encourage more domestic saving, investment and employment.

Methodology

Research design

In a research design, the steps of the study are laid out. Based on current events, analytic designs are created (Hennink, Hutter and Bailey, 2020). Case studies used a wide range of theories and data sources. This study made use of descriptive research methods. It allowed researchers to do a descriptive analysis on the study's variables. In the course of investigating, the origins and influences of a number of different variables were uncovered. Thus, it was possible for the researcher to conduct an exhaustive investigation and develop conclusions on a wide variety of subjects.

Qualitative research design is one technique to descriptive research design that was used in this study. Qualitative research projects accurately measure, display, and present data. It was also found that evidence and patterns in the subject were discovered using qualitative approaches. In the context of qualitative research, exploration is a common term. The architecture of the research allowed for the investigation and decryption of current theories and explanations. Being able to gain a new perspective on things is quite beneficial to me. Higher understanding and the discovery of new thoughts and ideas can be gained via the study of the topic (Moen and Middelthon, 2015). High-quality research like this makes good use of unstructured or semi-structured data collection methods. Qualitative research was conducted as a result of this.

The research approaches

This thesis was written using a qualitative research approach. Research in which explanation and description are the primary goals rather than quantitative data collection (Byrd, 2020). Researchers relied on descriptive information throughout the study to better understand social behavior in context. Researchers employed a qualitative data gathering strategy to understand more about social actors' behavior and how they see the term "mix." Since the research questions could not or should not be predetermined before to data collection, this method was used.

Data collection

Qualitative data was collected using exploratory data in order to facilitate future study. To collect data, the researcher needed to be conversant with the study keywords. Researchers are turning to pre-structured technologies and methods because they are concerned about the quality of the data they acquire. This study relied on a wide range of secondary sources, including textbooks, journals, the Internet, and previous research, to gather data. Once the data has been collected, the following step is to monitor it. The primary sources of information were newspapers, books, and the internet. This may be accomplished by depending on data that has previously been proven to be reliable and relevant. In order to conduct their work effectively, researchers must keep a close eye on all participants in the study and record everything they do. After a period of observation, a more in-depth investigation is conducted over a longer period of time. To gather data from one single source, long-term studies are necessary. It is the goal of this method to identify patterns in data that may be related to a collection of common qualities.

Data analysis

Understanding the two most prevalent qualitative data analysis methodologies is a good place to start when getting started with qualitative data analysis. Deductive reasoning begins with the evaluation of qualitative facts. The study questions and goals were used to examine the data. Because the researcher had a good understanding of what a representative sample would say, it was simple and quick to conduct. The induction method has no predefined boundaries or constraints. The researcher needs more time and resources to conduct a qualitative study of the data.

Strengths and weaknesses of the research method

Money saved: The researcher will examine data that has already been collected. Library visits will be necessary to gain knowledge and examine the work of others (Moen and Middelthon, 2015). It was also easy to locate secondary sources of information that were dependable, consistent, and precise. There may be some confidence in this information because it was gathered from previous research. Provide more in-depth details for the benefit of the readership. Some of the more difficult topics were easier to grasp for the researcher due to prior studies that had already covered them in detail. The new technology will allow for a slew of new methods for gathering private data. The method does not rely on just one or two studies to gather data, but rather on a large number of them.

Credibility of the research findings

According to the researcher, the findings might not be applied to a specific group or society. Due to the lack of participation, the results might not be extended to the entire community. It will be difficult to analyze the study because it might not fall into any of the usual categories. As a result, the research suffers from a number of additional issues. It takes longer for the researcher to gather data since he or she will be required to conduct extensive research in books, journals, and on the Internet. It will be necessary to spend more time interpreting the data and acquiring research-related information during the data collection phase than originally anticipated. Many investigations are needed in order to acquire enough data that may be regarded as reliable and real.

Findings

The success or failure of international currency use can be significantly affected by externalities. However, despite its quick development, RMB internationalization has had only a limited influence. This means that a worldwide or national economic impact assessment may be premature at this point. Having a forward-looking discussion on the benefits and expenses of the ongoing process is critical and possible.

There are several benefits for the PRC, particularly if the RMB becomes an international currency. By using the RMB as their invoicing and settlement currency, Chinese businesses may reduce transaction costs and reduce exchange risk. As with Mundell's investigation into the benefits of currency internationalization in decreasing exchange rate risks and transaction costs, the two are closely related. An estimate by the International Monetary Fund predicts that PRC trade would account for 11% of world trade by the end of 2014, up from 9% in 2010 (Wang, Ye and Li, 2017). While China is an important source of foreign direct investment (FDI) and a key destination for FDI, this trend will likely continue for a long time to come." There would still be a lot of interdependence between the PRC's economy and the global economy even if RMB internationalization had not occurred.

RMB's internationalization should benefit financial firms by decreasing currency mismatch. That means that many developing countries' "original sin" problem would be eliminated. As a result,

China's financial markets remain in their early stages. Growing ties between China and the global economy, particularly in the form of an open financial sector and internationalized banking, might lead to a worsening problem of currency mismatch. These institutions may be able to reduce the risk of currency exchange through RMB internationalization. Thus, BIS calculations of capital adequacy standards will be less influenced by the increasing weight of RMB-denominated assets held by financial institutions.

With the financial sector developing and becoming more sophisticated, the PRC's economic development model might be changed. Some people believe that financial development should come before currency globalization. Financial markets may expand in both breadth and depth by enlisting more participants and strengthening ties with the global financial market through the increased use of a local currency in international trade and investment. Hooy, Siong-Hook and Tze-Haw (2015) drew on Germany's and Japan's currency internationalization experiences to illustrate the importance of financial growth and the benefits that currency internationalization may provide. According to, currency internationalization would help both the domestic and global financial markets expand more quickly and efficiently. Based on the Economic and Monetary Union, private lending in euro-member countries rose 1.15 percent quicker than in other countries following the currency's internationalization.

Developing the financial market is viewed as a pre-requisite in the PRC for RMB internationalization. Instead, the financial industry might be propelled forward by the use of RMB-denominated foreign bond transactions and associated financial services as a result of widespread and deep RMB internationalization. Possibly, RMB internationalization will have a substantial influence on the Chinese bond market. According to numerous experts, the internationalization of the RMB will have a significant impact on Shanghai's development as a global financial center (Ren, Yang and Zhong, 2015). RMB internationalization might also act as a new push for financial reform if China considers that a more globally integrated currency is in the country's best interest.

Finally, RMB internationalization would allow Chinese businesses and financial institutions to borrow in RMB, lowering borrowing costs both ways. As a result of the growing foreign interest in RMB-denominated assets, Chinese businesses and financial institutions may borrow money on domestic financial markets at a lower cost. It is also possible for Chinese enterprises and financial institutions to receive loans or issue bonds in offshore RMB markets at lower prices if limitations on foreign borrowing are eased.. The PRC government would also be able to borrow more cheaply and run larger budget deficits if the RMB was made more widely accepted internationally. Alternatively, "monetary privilege or macroeconomic flexibility" can be used to describe this benefit (Hooy, Siong-Hook and Tze-Haw, 2015). By selling RMB-denominated government bonds and treasury bills, the PRC may secure low-cost financing from the rest of the world. This demographic shift will put a greater strain on the PRC's budgetary resources in the future. If the RMB is allowed to trade with other countries, the PRC may be able to find a new solution to these problems. Having a more sophisticated bond market in China might have a favorable influence on the country. If the PRC took advantage of this good circumstance and allowed its budget deficits to grow, it would be committing a tremendous mistake.

RMB internationalization would enable Chinese firms and financial institutions expand worldwide and increase China's foreign investment opportunities for the fourth time. Investing in one's own currency is more convenient and less expensive for most people since it is easier to keep track of. Due to a growth in foreign direct and indirect investment, future contracts and claims papers will increasingly employ the RMB as a currency for international transactions. Like the United States and Japan, the PRC's capital and financial accounts may show substantial deficits. US capital and financial account deficits grew quickly from 1953 to 1971; the deficit was 51.39 times bigger than the deficit in 1953. Similar to this, Japan's capital and financial accounts have been in deficit since 1981, when Japan began to encourage the worldwide use of the yen in its currency promotions. As of 1998, Japan has accumulated a debt of 21.35 trillion yen resulting from foreign investment.

While RMB internationalization may aid China's financial industry, it is not a sure thing. As the three main commercial banks in the People's Republic of China, China's three largest commercial banks, have risen to the top of the global banking industry in terms of assets, capital and profitability, they have become a worldwide powerhouse. Even as the domestic market has become more competitive, these financial institutions have been aggressively expanding their operations abroad.

Competition in the global financial markets will require that China's banks handle a growing number of RMB transactions in order to keep pace with international banks. It's realistic to assume that RMB internationalization will speed up the early stages of PRC financial institutions' worldwide development, particularly commercial banks.

Seigniorage from the rest of the world's currencies would be a little benefit if the RMB were to be made worldwide. The term "seigniorage" refers to the gap between a currency's nominal value and its manufacturing costs, which generates profit. By issuing a specific currency in exchange for goods and services, the government may earn a profit. Ren, Yang and Zhong (2015) pointed out that seigniorage consists of two parts: physical cash in the form of bank notes and coins, and financial claims priced in the local currency, respectively. Increasing the effective demand for assets decreases the interest rate on loans, which is what the latter is truly all about.

Reduced reliance on the US dollar is another advantage of RMB globalization. In light of China's rising market economy and volatile export sector, financial reform and liberalization of China's capital accounts is a top goal. Foreign exchange reserves are important for the People's Republic of China, but the country should exercise caution when building them up. So the PRC may have little choice but to hold large sums of US dollars, because it is clear that an over-reliance on US dollar-denominated assets not only provides low returns but is also harmful.

Developing countries must have a large amount of foreign currency on hand as a hedge against external shocks. A lack of currency-issuing capacity prevents poor countries' central banks from serving as lenders of last resort for foreign currencies. As quasi lenders of last resort, they can play a limited role if they have substantial overseas reserve reserves. Even if they have vast foreign reserves, they can only spend a small fraction of those cash during a crisis because they are afraid of losing their international reserves (Wang, Ye and Li, 2017). The globalization of the RMB and the emergence of the RMB as a key reserve currency in China may diminish China's dependence on the US dollar.

CONCLUSION

The RMB's impact on China's foreign exchange and economic growth was analyzed extensively in this research. The adoption of the RMB as an invoicing and settlement currency for PRC businesses may help them compete more effectively in international trade and investment. The transformational economic growth model of the PRC would benefit from a larger and more sophisticated financial sector as a result of RMB internationalization. Currency internationalization will help China's domestic financial industry flourish, not just worldwide but also in the People's Republic of China, according to empirical evidence. RMB internationalization may also enable enterprises and financial institutions in the PRC to borrow in RMB, perhaps saving them money in the process. Fourth, globalization would assist the expansion of Chinese firms and financial institutions overseas. If RMB internationalization is adopted, China's monetary authorities may collect seigniorage from foreign nations. To a greater extent, the seigniorage of the RMB will increase as the currency plays a larger role in trade agreements and becomes a more sought-after asset class. This might help China reduce its reliance on the US dollar and mitigate the welfare loss caused by low returns on offshore reserves," a researcher says. A last benefit of globalization is that China's political might will increase.

But RMB globalization comes at a cost, one that may or may not be mitigated over time, involving both long-term costs and short-term risks. RMB globalization may reduce China's monetary policy's effectiveness and independence, as well as the country's ability to decide on its own currency rate. The RMB's globalization effort is not without its risks. Because of this, the PRC's capacity to compete in the global economy may be harmed by asset bubbles and financial instability. These short-term hazards, however, can be avoided if the proper policy actions are implemented.

While RMB internationalization has its drawbacks, it is obvious that the benefits exceed the drawbacks. Having a competitive trade sector and a strong and sustainable economic growth are essential for the PRC to effectively execute RMB globalization. Domestic financial reforms must be accelerated first and foremost, particularly capital account liberalization. Reducing RMB market speculation is a last suggestion from this report. Increasing global and regional financial cooperation may help RMB internationalization.

The RMB's internationalization began in 2009, but so yet no relevant empirical research have been conducted. Aside from that, new and interesting things will be discovered as RMB globalization accelerates. We'll be searching for additional evidence of the advantages or costs of RMB internationalization, as well as strategies to overcome any obstacles that stand in the way and reduce any dangers that may occur.

REFERENCES OF RMB

Aloui, C., Hkiri, B., Hammoudeh, S. and Shahbaz, M., 2018. A multiple and partial wavelet analysis of the oil price, inflation, exchange rate, and economic growth nexus in Saudi Arabia. Emerging Markets Finance and Trade, 54(4), pp.935-956.

Barguellil, A., Ben-Salha, O. and Zmami, M., 2018. Exchange rate volatility and economic growth. Journal of Economic Integration, 33(2), pp.1302-1336.

Byrd, R., 2020. Qualitative research methods. Virtual Class, Memphis. Recuperado em, 17.

Cheng, L., Luo, J. and Liu, L., 2018. Is renminbi a (truly) international currency? An evaluation based on offshore foreign exchange market trading patterns. An Evaluation Based on Offshore Foreign Exchange Market Trading Patterns (October 9, 2018).

Chey, H.K. and Hsu, M., 2020. The impacts of policy infrastructures on the international use of the Chinese renminbi: A cross-country analysis. Asian Survey, 60(2), pp.221-244.

Chiang, T.C., 2022. Can gold or silver be used as a hedge against policy uncertainty and COVID-19 in the Chinese market?. China Finance Review International, (ahead-of-print).

Das, M.S., 2019. China's evolving exchange rate regime. International Monetary Fund.

Dieppe, A., Gilhooly, R., Han, J., Korhonen, I. and Lodge, D., 2018. The transition of China to sustainable growth–implications for the global economy and the euro area. ECB Occasional Paper, (206).

Duarte, A.P. and da Silva, N.B., 2022. Exchange Rate Synchronization for a Set of Currencies from Different Monetary Areas. Scientific Annals of Economics and Business.

Enderwick, P., 2018. The economic growth and development effects of China's One Belt, One Road Initiative. Strategic Change, 27(5), pp.447-454.

Guzman, M., Ocampo, J.A. and Stiglitz, J.E., 2018. Real exchange rate policies for economic development. World development, 110, pp.51-62.

Hennink, M., Hutter, I. and Bailey, A., 2020. Qualitative research methods. Sage.

Hooy, C.W., Siong-Hook, L. and Tze-Haw, C., 2015. The impact of the Renminbi real exchange rate on ASEAN disaggregated exports to China. Economic Modelling, 47, pp.253-259.

Huong, D.T.M., 2019. Real exchange rate and economic growth: An empirical assessment for Vietnam. Asian Economic and Financial Review, 9(6), pp.680-690.

Ibrahim, M. and Alagidede, P., 2018. Effect of financial development on economic growth in sub-Saharan Africa. Journal of Policy Modeling, 40(6), pp.1104-1125.

Iqbal, N., Fareed, Z., Shahzad, F., He, X., Shahzad, U. and Lina, M., 2020. The nexus between COVID-19, temperature and exchange rate in Wuhan city: new findings from partial and multiple wavelet coherence. Science of The Total Environment, 729, p.138916.

Ito, H. and McCauley, R.N., 2020. Currency composition of foreign exchange reserves. Journal of International Money and Finance, 102, p.102104.

Ji, Q., Liu, B.Y. and Fan, Y., 2019. Risk dependence of CoVaR and structural change between oil prices and exchange rates: A time-varying copula model. Energy Economics, 77, pp.80-92.

Jia, F., Shen, Y., Ren, J. and Xu, X., 2021. The impact of offshore exchange rate expectations on onshore exchange rates: The case of Chinese RMB. The North American Journal of Economics and Finance, 56, p.101349.

Jin, C., Wu, Z. and Yu, J., 2022, July. Analysis on the Influence of FED Interest Rate Adjustment on China's Economy. In 2022 2nd International Conference on Enterprise Management and Economic Development (ICEMED 2022) (pp. 1127-1135). Atlantis Press.

Kwan, C.H., 2018. Issues facing Renminbi internationalization: Observations from Chinese, regional and global perspectives. Public Policy Review, 14(5), pp.871-900.

Lengnoo, H. and Masih, M., 2018. Granger-causality between real exchange rate and economic growth: evidence from Thailand.

Ma, Y. and Wang, J., 2019. Co-movement between oil, gas, coal, and iron ore prices, the Australian dollar, and the Chinese RMB exchange rates: A copula approach. Resources Policy, 63, p.101471.

Maggiori, M., Neiman, B. and Schreger, J., 2019, May. The rise of the dollar and fall of the euro as international currencies. In AEA Papers and Proceedings (Vol. 109, pp. 521-26).

McDowell, D., 2019. The (Ineffective) Financial statecraft of China's bilateral swap agreements. Development and Change, 50(1), pp.122-143.

Mo, J., 2018. Land financing and economic growth: Evidence from Chinese counties. China Economic Review, 50, pp.218-239.

Moen, K. and Middelthon, A.L., 2015. Qualitative research methods. In Research in medical and biological sciences (pp. 321-378). Academic Press.

Pacheco Pardo, R., Knoerich, J. and Li, Y., 2019. The role of London and Frankfurt in supporting the internationalisation of the Chinese renminbi. New Political Economy, 24(4), pp.530-545.

Qian, Y., Liu, J. and Forrest, J.Y.L., 2022. Impact of financial agglomeration on regional green economic growth: evidence from China. Journal of Environmental Planning and Management, 65(9), pp.1611-1636.

Qin, F., Zhang, J. and Zhang, Z., 2018. RMB exchange rates and volatility spillover across financial markets in China and Japan. Risks, 6(4), p.120.

Ren, Y., Yang, Y. and Zhong, X., 2015, October. Effect of Currency Exchange Rate on Economic Growth Research Based on RMB Exchange Rate of VAR Model. In International Conference on

Education, Management and Information Technology (pp. 467-472). Atlantis Press.

Shaikh, E., Krishnan, D.E.E.P.I.K.A., Ahmed, F., Mishra, V.A.N.D.I.T.A. and Dagar, V., 2021. Exchange Rate, Stock Price and Trade Volume in US-China Trade War during COVID-19: An Empirical Study. Estudios de Economia Aplicada, 39(8).

Simtowe, M. and Yi, L., 2018. Evaluation of Effects of Real Exchange Rate on Economic Growth of Malawi: Empirical Analysis. World Journal of Innovative Research, 4(3), p.262486.

Sun, L., Xiang, M. and Marquez, L., 2019. Forecasting the volatility of onshore and offshore USD/RMB exchange rates using a multifractal approach. Physica A: Statistical Mechanics and its Applications, 532, p.121787.

Sun, R. and Park, C., 2021. INTERACTIONS BETWEEN THE EXCHANGE RATE OF RMB/USD IN THE ONSHORE AND OFFSHORE MARKETS: EVIDENCE FROM THE COMPARATIVE ANALYSIS ON '8.11'EXCHANGE RATE REFORM IN CHINA. International Journal of Economics and Finance Studies, 13(1), pp.318-339.

Umar, M. and Sun, G., 2018. Determinants of non-performing loans in Chinese banks. Journal of Asia Business Studies.

Vasani, S.A., Selvam, M. and Selvam, M., 2019. Relationship between real exchange rate and economic growth in India. ZENITH International Journal of Business Economics & Management Research, 9(3), pp.19-35.

Wang, Q. and Jiang, R., 2019. Is China's economic growth decoupled from carbon emissions. Journal of Cleaner Production, 225, pp.1194-1208.

Wang, S., Ye, S. and Li, X., 2017, July. The impact of real effective exchange rate volatility on economic growth in the process of renminbi internationalization an empirical study based on VAR model. In 2017 4th international conference on industrial economics system and industrial security engineering (IEIS) (pp. 1-7). IEEE.

Wang, Y.C., Tsai, J.J. and Chen, X., 2021. The impact of RMB internationalization and international situations on China's foreign exchange market: Dynamic linkages between USD/CNY and SDR/CNY. Emerging Markets Finance and Trade, 57(5), pp.1437-1454.

Xing, Y., 2019. How the iPhone widens the US trade deficit with China: The case of the iPhone X (No. 19-21). National Graduate Institute for Policy Studies.

Xu, J., 2022. Developments and implications of central bank digital currency: The case of China e-CNY. Asian Economic Policy Review.

Zhang, Q., Sornette, D. and Han, L., 2022. Evolutionary patterns of onshore and offshore Renminbi exchange rates with convexity–concavity indicators. Quantitative Finance, 22(2), pp.367-384.

Zhang, Y. and Zhang, S., 2018. The impacts of GDP, trade structure, exchange rate and FDI inflows on China's carbon emissions. Energy Policy, 120, pp.347-353.

Zucker-Marques, M. and da Silva, P.P., 2022. The Role of Institutions: A Cross-country Analysis of Renminbi Trading in Foreign Exchange Markets. China & World Economy, 30(3), pp.42-74.

CHAPTER 4
How Japan Achieved Economic Growth in the Past 50 Years

Economic growth and development are critical in promoting the wealth of a nation and increasing its powers and competitive advantage in the international market. Economic development enhances the distribution of resources. Economic growth deal with the production of good and services. These contribute to enhancing a nation's change in per capita income. Japanese economy during the pre-war era realized significant transformation in its structures and policies, which helped it become one of the most successful economies in the world (Ono, 2019). However, though the economy reached some point and started stagnating, the economic reforms which enhanced the revitalization of the economy to one of the most admired ones in the world make it a significant subject of study to understand the reasons which contributed to the growth of the company.

The transformation in Japan's economy was realized during post-world war II as the country addressed its challenges from World War II through restructuring and rebuilding its economic systems to recover the shattered economy. During World War II, the country was plunging into a massive debt crisis with the allies, such as the US, as they used the funds to promote its military for political powers and the need to strategically position its forces to gain a significant role in geopolitics during the war (Crawford, 1998). The increased spending on the military meant that the country did not undertake any significant economic investment and promoted the destruction of the country in terms of economy. The country experienced worse economic collapse since there was destruction in commercial and industrial buildings and many deaths, which hindered economic activities. It experiences challenges in domestic supply due to lack of production. The country experienced severe social problems, which resulted in chaos and high unemployment rates resulting in the abject poverty of its population. It also experienced the worst hunger issues due to food shortages and lack of production as many people were involved in the war.

However, the significant structural reforms undertaken by the Japanese government were able to promote economic growth. The country's economic growth was also enhanced through the collaboration and establishment of positive relationships with external forces such as its allies, which enabled the government to enhance critical and effective economic and cultural development. This helped it improve and sustain its economic growth. Japan's economic growth was enhanced through the Edo period during the Meiji period (Beckley, Horiuchi, and Miller, 2018). The institution laid the foundation for the realization of the country's long-term economic growth and development by addressing significant issues experienced during World War II, which negatively impacted the country's economy, such as inequalities. The paper examines the reasons for economic development in Japan over the past 50 years by undertaking a comprehensive literature review of different focuses which document the success of japan in promoting economic growth. However, the study anchors its examination through the three pillars of Japan's economic efficiencies, which include the goals set to catch up and surpass the western economy, such as the US economy. The second and third pillars include the role of large companies and a well-educated workforce. However, these pillars promote the key factors which facilitated the economic growth examined in the paper. These include the reduction in inequalities, technological development, and the ability of the Japanese government to shift from a semi-feudal structure to a modern, highly industrialized society and economy, the fiscal and industrial policies, and the National Comprehensive development plan of the country. These factors promoted the acceleration of competition in the Japanese economy. They led to the enhancement of new ideas that helped the economy to grow at an extraordinary speed and record better rates in its GDP and other elements of economic growth compared to western countries such as the USA and other Asian countries.

Literature review

Reducing inequalities.

According to Rios Serrano (2021), Japan was controlled by the ethnic-cultural settlement (Yamato), which became a kingdom of the warrior ruled through a centralized system and policy that made it possible to control the country's resources. This led to significant inequalities in the country as the aristocracy formed, which made the enhancement of trade difficult and impossible in their territory. These inequalities led to the emergence of monarchs across the country who controlled the factors of production, thus limiting the country's productivity and effective economic activities and investment. However, the tides changed during the Edo period when the feudal hereditary military dictatorship was abolished, bringing an end to the role of a capitalism-like economy in the modern, highly industrialized society (Ono, 2019). Under this regime, significant achievements were accomplished and contributed to the enhancement of Japan's economic growth as they helped establish the foundation of economic growth. During this period, the government could promote agricultural production and enhance wealth distribution by returning the land to peasants, which increased the country's economic capacity. The agrarian reforms helped the country undertake economic activities through trade which attracted foreign investment and laid a foundation for promoting raw material production for their industries. This empowered the labor force and increased the nation's wealth, which contributed to the increase in its gross domestic product.

The government also reduced inequalities in the country by abolishing social hierarchies and stratification. According to (Rios Serrano, 2021), the government removed restrictions on the business environment. It provided the ability for the financial institution to undertake their activities, which linked to huge industries and businesses and enhanced stock ownership, promoting financial strength in the country.

These improvements enhanced the development and increased market share among the country, the industrialist, and business people. This generated an enormous capital formation and cash flow, enabling the government to undertake significant economic development that helped the country become an economic juggernaut that surpassed the achievement of the superpowers such as the USA. However, the country's economic prowess stagnated due to different circumstances and the dependence on particular policies, leading to negative impacts. Their status in the global world faded, but the lesson from Japan's economic reforms and transformation should be emulated and considered to help avoid recession. Especially in this period, the country and the global economy are experiencing severe financial challenges affecting the global population.

In order to reduce the inequalities in the country, the government made a significant investment in the reduction system whereby they trained and educated the labor force. This made it critical for economic growth as the government ensured that they had skilled and experienced labor in undertaking the reaction activities and promoting the enhancement of new ideas in the economy. Education was a fundamental tool for the economic growth and development in the country as it was able to cope with the economic activities and development of the European countries by adopting western ethics and eastern science.

Also, as the government enhanced the reduction of inequalities, it ensured that it utilized the educated labor force towards contributing to the increase in GDP by developing the primary industry such as steel plants. The increased education in the country led to increased innovation with the introduction of new products and new investors in the industrial sectors, which helped spearhead the transformation in the society through the development of infrastructures. Many of the development in the industrial sectors were enhanced to target the international market and exploit the incredible opportunities accrued from the market. They contributed to the Japanese companies increasing their competitive advantage and efficiency as they struggled to keep up with the international competition. They copied the production design, and through the rise of innovative production techniques, the companies were able to produce superior products and services that competed well in the international market. Education increased the labor force capacity, and the country created a pool of well-dedicated and committed employees through cultural transformation. Most of the employees were youths. Since the country had a considerable population, it had access to cheaper labor and a vast supply that enhanced the high volume of economic production. Most of the employees were willing and were motivated to work hard and for extra hours. Also, the country integrated the culture of good behaviors by encouraging the schools to teach the students the rigid roles of behaviors such as the choreographed submissive posture, which helped the labor force enhance good manners and also have effective customer relations and discipline which promoted the growth and development of the Japan economy.

Promoting equality in society is critical for enhancing a country's economy since it encourages the development of power, prosperity, and wealth. Japan ensured that they promoted equality in the country by providing unrestricted rights to property which accelerated economic growth in specific economic sectors. Removal of inequalities also promotes cohesion in the country, creating an enabling business environment that attracts more investment and brings foreign direct investment to the country. Also, this strategy enhanced the competition in the labor force and among communities, making it easy for the government to distribute and allocate resources as cohesion and equality reduced conflict in resource sharing and utilization.

Technological development

The extensive education reforms undertaken in the country were critical for economic development and growth. These reforms enhanced the essential foundation of technology development by empowering people with skills and knowledge to develop new ideas. Their analytical skills and proper attention to rules were enhanced and promoted. The country sprung into the rapid development of technology, and the business institution started utilizing and integrating technology in their operation and activities, resulting in increased production efficiency and effectiveness (Beckley, Horiuchi, and Miller, 2018). Improved technology infrastructure and technological advancement are critical for economic development since it ensures that the production activities are enhanced efficiently, and the country can promote quality production and constant supply of the goods and services in the market. Companies started utilizing effective management practices through the use of technology and also enhanced the utilization of human resource management, which increased the productivity and performance of the workforce. Technological utilization during post-world war II increased in Japan as the country made it possible for business institutions to integrate robots, computer chips, and software into manufacturing (Crawford, 1988)). This promoted competitiveness in the market and made it easy for Japan manufactured goods to compete in the international market as they were of good quality. They promoted the relatively low cost of production. This meant that they sold their goods at a relatively low price in the international market compared to the other products, which increased their demand and led to increased foreign exchange for the country, which they utilized in promoting economic investment. Infrastructure development is critical to encourage the increase in national output and gross domestic production since it depends on the high government expenditures towards economic activities and initiatives.

The fiscal and industrial policies

The government of Japan spearheaded economic growth through the provision of incentives to the institution through the tax breaks to the promising sectors, which enabled them to undertake business activities effectively. Also, the government protected local businesses and industries through trade barriers and exchange rates, discouraging imports but promoting exports (Beckley, Horiuchi, and Miller, 2018). The government also provided the business institution with cheap credit and administrative guidance. The cheap credit to the business institution enhanced the formulation of capital and could spearhead investment by ensuring that the institution had access to financial support. The government ensured that it promoted the accessibility of the critical factors of production in enhancing economic growth and development through investment and capital accessibility. Cheap credits motivated institutions to access loans from financial institutions, and the increased demand for the loans increased the financial institution such as banks and provided the link between big companies and the economic growth and development of the country.

According to Crawford (1998), Japan experienced a 7.1% annual increase in GDP from 1945 to 1958 and a 9.5% yearly increase from 1959 to1970. Due to this GDP increase, the Japanese economy rose to prominent ranks in the global economy ranking and competed with the economic status of Americans. However, this tremendous increase was because of the increase in government policies, which helped create a diversified economy. Japan enhanced the development of its economy through an export-led economy and trade which only concentrated on the exportation of goods. This made it possible to develop and sustain their local business and industries while restricting imports to protect the domestic economy by limiting the influence of foreign externalities in the economy.

The country also forged good relationships with the US after a period of conflict, which saw the country shift to the communist countries for trade exploration but later shifted to the US relationship. Thus relationship played a role in spearheading the growth and development of the Japanese economy, which was considered an integral policy in the period. The relationship ensured that the country could finance its operation through the low-interest loans advanced by the American government as they sought to strengthen its ties with Japan to have their geopolitical influence in the Asian countries (Beckley, Horiuchi, and Miller, 2018). The flow of capital and direct investment from America made it possible for the Japanese government to overcome capital challenges for domestic investments. The much-needed capital enabled the spearheading of economic activities, which saw the doubling of Japan's loans from an institution such as the World Bank in the subsequent years starting from 1958.

Conversely, using the standard economic growth model, it is critical to appreciate the significance of capital injection in the domestic economy for spurring economic growth and development. The capital injection helps strengthen the economy by investing in developing economic infrastructures. Japan prioritized its private sector development, which plays a critical role in economic growth through increasing GDP by promoting productivity. Also, the export-led economy helped the country deal with the balance of trade deficiency experienced in the mid-1950s (Beckley, Horiuchi, and Miller, 2018). The USA relationship made it possible for the country to access the market. Due to the fear of the American government losing its grip on the Asian country through Japan finding economic accommodation from the communist bloc, they removed protectionist policies, opening the US market for Japanese goods. When President Eisenhower led, the US government reduced the tariffs by 20%, making the Japanese goods more accessible to the American market and consumers and increasing their foreign exchange. This helped in dealing with the balance of trade deficiency, thus enabling the country to undertake significant economic development investments that spearheaded the economic growth. According to Beckley, Horiuchi, and Miller (2018) US market absorbed more than 30% of the Japanese goods boosting Japan's export. From 1958-1960 the country was able to realize its first ever trade surplus as its export of manufactured goods to America increased by 150%.

Labor Force

According to Vittorio (2012), Japan was able to experience excellent results through mobilizing the labor force to shift from low productivity sectors and increasing their participation in the high productivity sectors and the use of skilled labor in industry and modern services. This shift made it easy for the country to convert its production by achieving mass production, which promoted economies of scale that provided opportunities to the country and made them leverage the opportunities in the international market (Vittorio, 2012). The shift enabled the country to increase productivity, wages, aggregate demand, and employment. The labor force efficiency was promoted by labor mobility and the extensive labor absorption of jobs created by the enhancement of the large companies and small firms. The large companies enhanced the high productivity, which led to increased wages and stable employment, while the small business enhanced the lower labor costs (Vittorio, 2012). The two sectors were able to increase productivity and utilize the advancement in improving the labor investment by the government through increased education and training, which increased the labor force's skills, making it easy and efficient to leverage the technological advancements.

According to Horiuchi (2011), the country was able to increase the longevity length of the population, thus making it possible to contribute to the massive population of the labor force which provided labor in the country. The economic growth in the country during post-world war II was able to oversee an increase in the country's life expectancy. The labor force is critical in the enhancement of economic growth and development. The country managed a decline in the mortality rate, thus ensuring that the industries supplied a steady flow of labor in the market. The Japanese population enhanced their health, which increased their life expectancy and improved the labor force's productivity in the market. According to Horiuchi (2011), the Japanese population's health concerns and personal hygiene were enhanced through the historical influence of Chinese medicine. The use of Chinese medicine enhanced the healthy lifestyles of the Japanese people, which made it possible for the population to stay healthy for a long time without suffering from chronic illness, which affected the labor supply and the diminishing power and returns of the labor force. Japan has effective social stratification, which makes it possible to communicate and interact in society effectively. High levels of homogeneity in the community contribute to the high communicative quality and cultural equality (Horiuchi, 2011). These aspects enhanced economic growth since they promoted human relations, enabling the government to institute and utilize human capital to promote economic growth.

National Comprehensive development plan of the country

The economic growth was realized through the achievement of the government and the different regimes to shift from a semi-feudal structure to a modern, highly industrialized society and economy (Rios Serrano, 2021). This increased the economic and industrial revolution in the country, contributing to the increase in production in the country. On the other hand, Japanese consumers accepted high prices and scarce credit. The government influenced the financial market through significant reforms and policies. The government set the ten-year sustainable target goals, which were aimed at enhancing the government to achieve a balance of development in public policy, monetary policy, and fiscal policy. According to Rios Serrano (2021), the long-term and short-term plans from the Japanese government enhanced the growth of the private sector, which was critical in rooting the country's economic growth.

Also, according to Bhuiyan (2019), numerous comprehensive development plans were undertaken by the Japanese government, which contributed to the development and growth of the economy as witnessed during post-World War II. Japan was mainly affected by World War II, whereby most of the infrastructure was affected by the nuclear bombing. Therefore to promote development and increase productivity in the economy, the country promoted the development of the labor mobilization plan. This was supposed to allocate labor in critical industries, which the government had identified as an effective investment to increase the country's economic activities. The government changed labor allocation and increased it towards the munition industry (Bhuiyan, 2019). The empowerment of labor was realized through the unionization of labor. This provided it with the ability to champion its needs. This led to increased labor wages as the labor market and unions set high salaries, which would benefit the population by improving living standards and increasing the population's consumption power, which promoted demand increase. The increase in demand led to the development and growth of the different industries as they increased production to meet the high demand for goods and services. This promoted the development and growth of the economy. Also, the increased demand meant that the government revenue increased through the increase in their taxable money as the industries recorded an increase in revenue which they remitted a significant share to the government. The increase in government revenue increased the government's ability to undertake investment opportunities in the country, promoting economic development. Also, the population increased investment through their income and enhanced their savings in financial institutions such as banks, which increased their capital for investment. This plan had a series of positive impacts on the economy, contributing to the realization of the rapid economic growth in Japan.

Methodology

The study was enhanced through the literature review of both qualitative and quantitative articles. The articles were carefully selected, with only the research with credible information about the subject matter included in the study. The data was collected using secondary data from the various research articles covering

Japan's economic growth for the past 50 years. Also, the data collected was mainly historical data from government institutions and was utilized in undertaking the analysis and the significant conclusion of the factors which led to the increase and growth of the japan economy during the post-world war II. The need for using qualitative and quantitate data was enhanced due to the nature of the research, which was hard to undertake primary research and conduct a survey or observational research. Therefore the two studies provided extensive information for the study and contributed to a huge study population involving the different studies. The findings were examined through a literature review analysis. Most of the research highlighted similarities in their finding, which results in the credibility and reliability of the information.

The study was also promoted through the use of the interpretive framework. This helps in accounting for the gaps in the research utilized in the study. The literature review is undertaken from numerous qualitative and quantitative research articles, which provide insights on the growth of the Japanese economy during the post-world war II period and also provide the economic trends and situation after the economic growth and current period.

The articles used in the research discussed different concepts. Some aspects reviewed in the study include the rapid longevity extension in postwar Japan. Understanding the reason for longevity is critical. They are highly correlated to the success and increase in Japan's labor force, which contributed to the country's economic growth as it contributed to the rise in productivity and ensured increased demand for the goods and services produced in the country. Also, some articles covered the government roles and fiscal policies that contributed to Japan's economic growth. It is critical to factor in all the factors enhanced in the different articles and single in the most high-ranking articles, which have been addressed numerous times in the utilized articles. The analysis was also undertaken through statistical analysis. This enhanced the establishment of the relationship of the factors. It determined their accuracy by accounting for the freedom of error and the variance in discussing the factors contributing to economic growth.

Data analysis

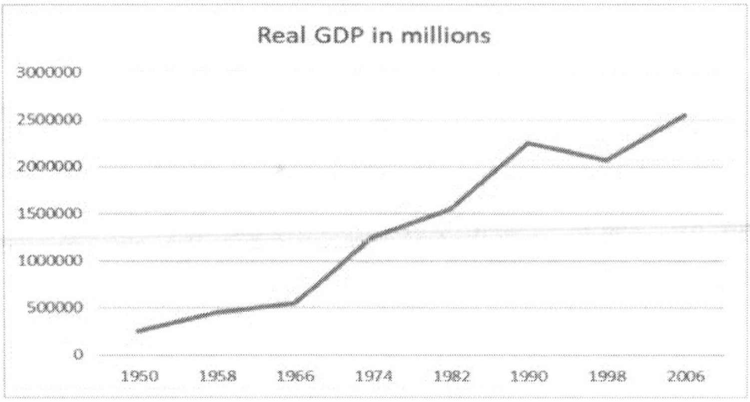

Fig 1: Real GDP in millions

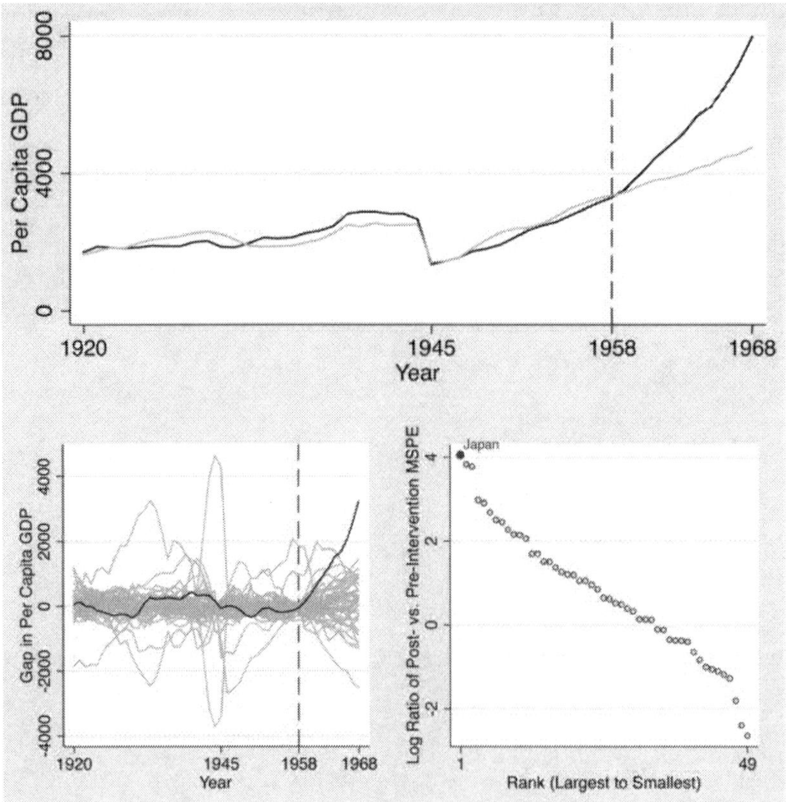

Fig: 2: Per Capita GDP

During the economic growth period, Japan was able to realize a high growth rate by realizing a growth of 9.9%real GDP per annum. The data indicates that the economy in the country was increasing each year as the GDP kept growing. The resulting factors in the growth of GDP were enormous as the change contributed to the increase in employment, consumption, and productivity. Japan had increased economic investment and enhanced the private sector's growth and development, which was critical in promoting the high growth rate in GDP. According to Vittorio (2012), the impact of the increase in GDP was the ability of the country to mobilize its labor force and produce excellent results such as efficiency and effectiveness in productivity and performance in the industrial industries.

	(Actual) Japan	Synthetic Japan
Post-war Economic Recovery	2.330	2.179
Post-war Population Growth	1.201	1.179
Per capita GDP (1920–1957 average)	2,175.99	2,176.82
Per capita GDP (1944)	2,658.97	2,497.22
Per capita GDP (1958)	3,288.90	3,346.16
Member of U.N. in 1945	0	0.147

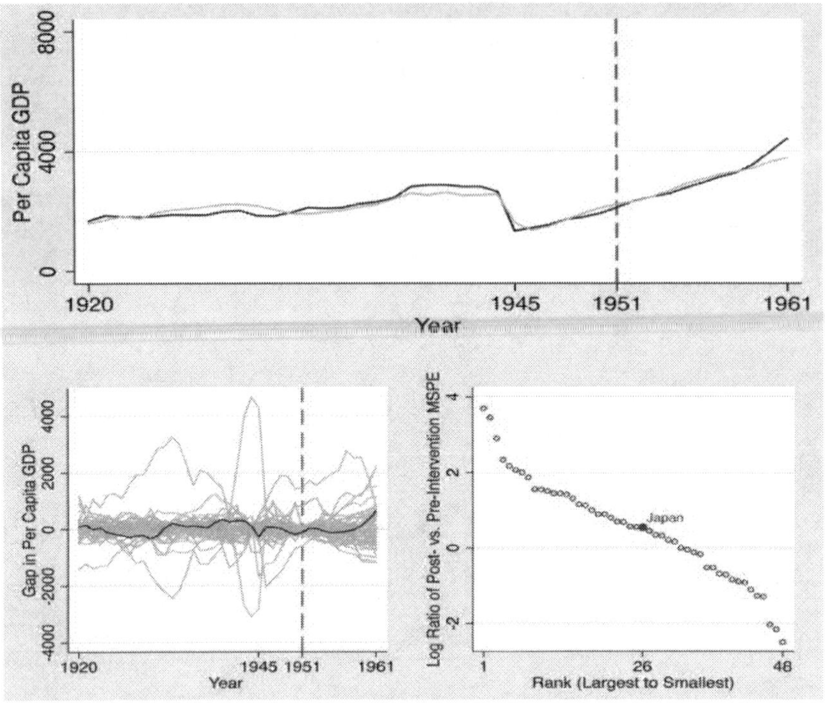

According to Beckley, Horiuchi, and Miller (2018), Japan's per capita GDP grew at 9.3% per annum from 1958 to 1968. It recorded an increase in GDP from $3289 to $7983. This increase was enhanced through the increased engagement with the US. Without the engagement, the country's GDP would have been reduced by an average of $1288 annually, equating to a gap of 39.2% of the 1958 level (Beckley, Horiuchi, and Miller, 2018). The USA relationship made it possible for the country to access the market.

Due to the fear of the American government losing its grip on the Asian country through Japan finding economic accommodation from the communist bloc, they removed protectionist policies, opening the US market for Japanese goods. When President Eisenhower led, the US government reduced the tariffs by 20%, making the Japanese goods more accessible to the American market and consumers and increasing their foreign exchange. This helped in dealing with the balance of trade deficiency, thus enabling the country to undertake significant economic development investments that spearheaded the economic growth.

'The increase in economic growth in Japan was enhanced due to the increased wealth holding of households. According to Ono (2019), the increased households in the country resulted in higher consumption which increased demand and also contributed to higher production in the country, contributing to an increase in the GDP and income per capita of the Japanese population. The expanded wealth holding in the country resulted from increased employment and investment. The government must increase investment and spending in job creation to increase the region's employment rates. Higher employment rates increase the income of the population and consumption, which increase the money supply making it easy for investment since the consumption increases government revenue through taxation of the consumption goods. The government had undertaken significant measures and policies promoting efficient resource allocation and utilization. Resource allocation is critical in promoting equality and economic growth since it determines which sectors the government aims to develop more than others. Though it is crucial to enhance the development of all industries equally, one sector can disadvantage the economy in terms of the balance of trade. Investment in the agricultural sector and lack of investment in the industrial sector means that the main export will be the farm produce which collects low returns in tern of foreign revenue due to their low prices compared to the industrial and manufactured products and services. Therefore the Japanese government increased the development of the industry. This increased productivity, and through the expansion of the market in the USA for their good and services, the country was able to enhance and promote favorable terms of trade whereby they collected a huge amount of returns from the export hence promoting the increase in GDP.

Also, the government increased investment in education and training through education reforms. Through this investment, the Japanese government raised the knowledge and skills in the labor force, contributing to technological advancement and productivity. According to Vittorio (2012), the average years of education for people aged 156-64 were 9.1 in 1950 compared to the USA, 11.3, and Germany, 10.4. However, the statistics compared to the Netherlands were 8.1 and 9. In France. The indicator in 1973 was 12.1 years. This indicates an increase from 1950, demonstrating the significance of the education reforms in contributing to economic growth. Numerous researches have established a relationship between the rise in education reforms through the increase in education and training with the expansion and increased growth rates in GDP.

Similarly, Japan recorded a low disparity in the Gini coefficient, which indicates that the population was less exposed to a vulnerability which enabled the government to undertake effective policies in promoting economic growth. In order to reduce the inequalities in the country, the government made a significant investment in the reduction system whereby they trained and educated the labor force. This made it critical for economic growth as the government ensured that they had skilled and experienced labor in undertaking the reaction activities and promoting the enhancement of new ideas in the economy. Education was a fundamental tool for the economic growth and development in the country as it was able to cope with the economic activities and development of the European countries by adopting western ethics and Eastern science.

CONCLUSION

Consequently, the Japanese economy experienced rapid growth from 1950-1973 but plunged into a slow rate of growth and stagnation, followed by significant economic challenges from the structural crisis. The three pillars of Japan's economic efficiencies include the goals set to catch up and surpass the western economy, the role of large companies, and a well-educated workforce. However, these pillars promote the key factors which facilitated economic growth. These factors enabled the acceleration of competition in the Japanese economy. It led to the enhancement of new ideas that helped the economy to grow at an extraordinary speed and record better rates in its GDP and other elements of economic growth compared to western countries such as the USA and other Asian countries. The economic growth was also realized through the achievement of the government and the different regimes to shift from a semi-feudal structure to a modern, highly industrialized society and economy. The government set the ten-year sustainable target goals, which were aimed at enhancing the government to achieve a balance of development in public policy, monetary policy, and fiscal policy.

The capital injection helps strengthen the economy by investing in developing economic infrastructures. Japan prioritized its private sector development, which plays a critical role in economic growth through increasing GDP by promoting productivity. Also, the export-led economy helped the country deal with the balance of trade deficiency experienced in the mid-1950s. The USA relationship made it possible for the country to access the market.

Economic growth deal with the production of good and services. These contribute to enhancing a nation's change in per capita income. Japanese economy during the pre-war era realized significant transformation in its structures and policies, which helped it become one of the most successful economies in the world (Ono, 2019). However, though the economy reached some point and started stagnating, the economic reforms which enhanced the revitalization of the economy to one of the most admired ones in the world make it a significant subject of study to understand the reasons which contributed to the growth of the company.

Though the country promoted the export-led economy, many opportunities and benefits in fostering economic growth were realized through the input of internal factors. Export-led trade and the economy also catalyzed economic growth since it promoted the critical element of efficiency in production and operation in the economy. Japan was able to catch up with other

European countries, such as the USA, through their Japan model, which enhanced technological advancement and supported the economic investment in promoting the growth of industries and trade. The country promoted an effective relationship between the government and business, which increased development as the government undertook significant policies supporting the business enterprises. The enhancement of the favorable business environment increased investment as the investors could leverage the relaxation of numerous taxes and experienced government incentives, reducing production costs and increasing their profits. Also, the government initiatives ensured that the industries were equipped with the right technology and labor skills to perform operations and increase productivity, which enabled the companies to compete in the international market. This increased the competition of Japanese industries and products and services, which promoted the increase in consumption which was also supported by the rise in demand as the income levels of the population increased due to high wages and increased employment rates.

The tremendous economic growth achieved by Japan within a short period has encouraged numerous East Asian countries who have enhanced their integration of the Japan success factors in promoting economic expansion and venturing into the global markets. Many countries seek to exploit the benefits of establishing strong trade and investment linkages with the European countries since Japan's economic growth success factors were enhanced by the vast loans accrued from the good relationships with the USA.

However, the institutions and governments emulating the Japanese success factors should consider their economy, the factors of production involved, and the situation surrounding their investment to realize the full opportunities and benefits from the relationships. This is because the benefits realized by Japan have come to hurt and harm the economy of Japan. These are not addressed in the study. The government undertakes the success factors and initiatives to promote economic growth but, in the long run, produces adverse effects which have led to the stagnation of Japan's economic growth, resulting in considerable adverse effects.

Nevertheless, Japan's growth abilities indicate that there is a need for the government to undertake significant reforms to achieve the goals and objectives of the economy. The reforms ensured that the country could reduce the weakness in its domestic policies and enhanced the reduction of external vulnerabilities in the economy. This process and the success factors exploit the opportunities and benefits of strengthening the domestic market and exploring the international market opportunities. Industrial activities and investment are also critical for enhancing economic growth and development. The government of Japan spearheaded economic growth through the provision of incentives to the institution through the tax breaks to the promising sectors, which enabled them to undertake business activities effectively. Also, the government protected local businesses and industries through trade barriers and exchange rates, discouraging imports but promoting exports. The government also provided the business institution with cheap credit and administrative guidance.

The government ensured that it promoted the accessibility of the critical factors of production in enhancing economic growth and development through investment and capital accessibility. Japan prioritized its private sector development, which plays a crucial role in economic growth through increasing GDP by promoting productivity.

The increased education in the country led to increased innovation with the introduction of new products and new investors in the industrial sectors, which helped spearhead the transformation in the society through the development of infrastructures. Many of the development in the industrial sectors were enhanced to target the international market and exploit the incredible opportunities accrued from the market, making the

Japanese companies increase their competitive advantage and efficiency.

Also, the export-led economy helped the country deal with the balance of trade deficiency experienced in the mid-1950s. Promoting equality in society is critical for enhancing a country's economy since it encourages the development of power, prosperity, and wealth. Japan ensured that they promoted equality in the country by providing unrestricted rights to property which accelerated economic growth in specific economic sectors. Removal of inequalities also promotes cohesion in the country, creating an enabling business environment that attracts more investment and brings foreign direct investment to the country.

The extensive education reforms undertaken in the country were critical for economic development and growth. These reforms enhanced the essential foundation of technology development by empowering people with skills and knowledge to develop new ideas. Their analytical skills and proper attention to rules were enhanced and promoted. Foreign technology acquisition was significant for the development of the Japanese economy. Increased technology infrastructure and technological advancement are critical for economic development since it ensures that the production activities are enhanced efficiently, and the country can promote quality production and constant supply of the goods and services in the market.

Companies started utilizing effective management practices through the use of technology and also enhanced the utilization of human resource management, which increased the productivity and performance of the workforce. Technological utilization during post-world war II increased in Japan as the country made it possible for business institutions to integrate robots, computer chips, and software into manufacturing (HB). This promoted competitiveness in the market and made it easy for Japan manufactured goods to compete in the international market as they were of good quality.

RECOMMENDATION

The three pillars of Japan's economic efficiencies include the goals set to catch up and surpass the western economy, the role of large companies, and a well-educated workforce. However, these pillars promote the key factors which facilitated economic growth. However, while praising the economic development of Japan through the utilization of the success factors, it is critical to ensure that we investigate and evaluate how the success factors and policies increased adverse problems in the country. After experiencing the growth, Japan is facing economic challenges due to the economic stagnation which has characterized the country for a long time, making it hard to enhance its development beyond the realized development and growth of post-world war II. According to Ono (2019), the increase in consumption in Japan due to the government role and the fiscal and monetary policies which promoted economic growth led to demand shortages as the economy stagnated since the financial assets were increased and stopped increasing, affecting the economy. Future research should improve their assessment of how the policies affected the country. Also, future research should address how Japan can enhance and revive economic growth through increasing demand by using effective monetary and fiscal policies. Studies should ensure that they improve understanding of the specific monetary and fiscal policies applicable to Japan's economic stagnation issues without causing further economic challenges. The problems are complex since Japan is experiencing a high employment rate but stagnation in its consumption and GDP.

Consumption stagnation is a serious issue since it reduces economic investment opportunities and productivity. The effect of the problem is a reduction in the country's capital formation, thus lacking revenue, which leads to a deficit in their budget as they seek to enhance their investment and government expenditure through undertaking loans. This also culminates in risking the problem of high-interest rates and inflation which increases the rise of commodities prices, thus reducing the consumption in the economy and eventually affecting employment and the quality of labor production since the wages will reduce. Therefore for the Japanese government to realize the economic growth experienced in the previous years, they should consider increasing employment through public employment and government purchase which increases demand in the country. However, the continued use of fiscal and monetary policies to stimulate consumption will continue to have negative complications since one benefit results in other negative issues, reducing the impact of the policies utilized in reviving the economic stagnation. However, researchers should also examine the effects of increasing public employment and government purchase to stimulate consumption increase in the economy.

Conversely, while addressing the factor success that promoted the economic growth in Japan, the researcher has overlooked the significance of the Korean War. The Korean War also promoted numerous advantages and opportunities for Japan in economic trade, enabling them to spearhead economic growth. Future research should ensure that they investigate the contribution of the Korean War since it provided the country and other East Asian countries with the opportunities such as creating a vast and strong demand for goods and services. The Korean War was advanced to enhance the military efforts of the USA as they sought to conquer the Asian region. These goods and services were promoted to supply the military with basic needs and equipment, which were essential in winning the war. This ensured that the country could expand its economy by entering the global marketplace through the success accrued from the Korean War.

Political stability's role in stimulating continuous improvement and technological progress was not examined extensively in the research, thus limiting the study's limitation as the success factors were limited. This results in a lack of a comprehensive understanding of what led to the economic growth in Japan.

However, future research can include the contribution of Japan's political stability toward economic development.

This led to economic stability by making it possible for the business enterprises to undertake their activities. It also promoted the establishment of an effective relationship between the government and the business. The discussion about political stability is critical due to the contribution of the different regimes in Japan. Japan was ruled by many regimes which instituted different cultures in the society, leading to the development of institutions that promoted economic growth. The economic growth is attributed to the contribution of different regimes, such as the Meiji era and the Edo regime, which marked the modernization of the Japanese economic system resulting in numerous agrarian reforms. The tides changed during the Edo period when the feudal hereditary military dictatorship was abolished, bringing an end to the role of a capitalism-like economy towards the modern, highly industrialized society. Under this regime, significant achievements were accomplished and contributed to the enhancement of Japan's economic growth as they helped establish the foundation of economic growth. During this period, the government could promote agricultural production and enhance wealth distribution by returning the land to peasants, which increased the country's economic capacity.

The role of the military defeat by America should be evaluated extensively using the historical data and the available modern data to provide a comprehensive analysis of the situation and determine its impact on Japan. It increased the desire to reach the development of many European countries and the tendency to emulate the American model. This increased the technological advancement in the country as Japan copied most of the American technologies and improved them, which made it possible for the country to surpass the American economy in many sectors of the industry. The USA relationship made it possible for the country to access the market. Due to the fear of the American government losing its grip on the Asian country through Japan finding economic accommodation from the communist bloc, they removed protectionist policies, opening the US market for Japanese goods. When President Eisenhower led, the US government reduced the tariffs by 20%, making the Japanese goods more accessible to the American market and consumers and increasing their foreign exchange.

The impact of the USA-Japan relationship has had negative implications for its structural reforms and culture. The relationship expanded the Japanese goods market by removing tariffs and increasing FDI, which boosted economic growth. They have had a negative impact which should be addressed significantly since the intentions of the USA were to enhance their efforts in keeping Japan in its sphere of influence. Scholars should analyze how this strategic move by the Americans has impacted the continued growth and sustainability of the economic development of Japan and its expansion. However, foreign technology acquisition was significant for developing the Japanese economy.

Consequently, consumption stagnation is a serious issue since it reduces economic investment opportunities and productivity. Therefore for the Japanese government to realize the economic growth experienced in the previous years, they should consider increasing employment through public employment and government purchase which increases demand in the country. The continued use of fiscal and monetary policies to stimulate consumption will continue to have negative complications since one benefit results in other negative issues, reducing the impact of the policies utilized in reviving the economic stagnation.

REFERENCE LIST JAPANESE ECONOMY

Beckley, M., Horiuchi, Y. and Miller, J., 2018. AMERICA'S ROLE IN THE MAKING OF JAPAN'S ECONOMIC MIRACLE. Journal of East Asian Studies, 18(1), pp.1-21.

Bhuiyan, M.Z.A., (2019). The Japanese economy's miracle after the Second World War (WW2).

Crawford, R., 1998. Reinterpreting the Japanese Economic Miracle. [online] Harvard Business Review. Available at: <https://hbr.org/1998/01/reinterpreting-the-japanese-economic-miracle> [Accessed 13 July 2022].

Horiuchi, S., 2011. Major causes of the rapid longevity extension in postwar Japan. The Japanese journal of population, 9(1), p.162.

Ono, Y., 2019. Japanese Economy: Two Lost Decades and How Many More?. [online] Intereconomics. Available at: <https://www.intereconomics.eu/contents/year/2019/number/5/article/japanese-economy-two-lost-decades-and-how-many-more.html> [Accessed 13 July 2022].

Rios Serrano, E., 2021. An Economic Miracle in East Asia? The Case of Japan in the Post-War Period: Korean War Dichotomies and the Effect of Industrial Policies and Strong Fiscal Institutions as Causes for Long-Term Economic. International Journal of Scientific and Research Publications (IJSRP), 11(3), pp.47-55.

Vittorio, V., 2012. Growth and crisis in the Japanese economy (No. 201207). The University of Turin.

CHAPTER 5
German Economic Miracle

Germany recovered from the devastation of World War II through an alleged "economic miracle" that started in 1948. West Germany's economic system became one of the most recognized in the world due to its subsequent development and stability. However, it began to experience pressures in the 1990s, which were made worse by the expenses of unification (Janik, 142). Through various economic policies, programs, and strategic implementations, Germany grew (overall) to what it is today.

Before the war, Germany had been a nation that was struggling for power. The country's unique geography meant that trade could only be maintained by water. Nevertheless, there were substantial improvements in technology and industrialization during the late 19th century; during this period, the German Empire became an economic power widely admired throughout Europe (Scherner et al., 1000). The financial crisis of the early 1920s devastated Germany, and the nation's political system was on the brink of collapse. Effective economic administration contributed significantly to Germany's impressive economic performance, but temporary factors significantly boosted economic growth immediately following World War II. Notably, a sizable labour population of unemployed people returned troops, and displaced people were available, eager to start again and ready to work long hours for pay, leaving their employers with a sizeable investment surplus.

West Germany's gross national product (GNP) increased by 8% a year between 1951 and 1961, which is twice as fast as Britain, the United States, and nearly twice as quickly as France. Exports also tripled during this period. Even during brief economic downturns (such as the 1973–74 oil crisis), West Germany's economy continued to grow (Gilpin, 324). West Germany's economy had been experiencing a cycle of a business boom since the early 1980s and had continued into 1992 when East and West Germany reunited 1990. Germany was an international trade powerhouse and one of the world's sizeable schemes. All of this was accomplished while keeping interest rates low. In the 2000s, Germany had an increase in economic growth. In 2002 the level of unemployment was chronically high, and the ageing German population was another problem which led to the welfare system being considered (Dustmann et al., 167).

Most analysts concur that human resources, physical capital, natural resources, and technology impact economic development and growth. Governments in highly advanced countries prioritize these issues (Ouoba, 101635). Since the early 1970s, Germany's economy had started to run into a few problems that made it difficult to achieve further growth. A free market economic system was designed and implemented in an unstable environment of high unemployment and high inflation. The advent of powerful computers and the internet brought more competition among companies to sell products. However, there was also a substantial social acceptance for the reunification of East and West Germany, leading to investments in eastern Germany that created jobs for returning GDR residents (Ragnitz, 25).

Technological advancement

The most crucial reason for Germany's economic expansion from the 1970s to 2020 was its technological advancement. According to the report, Germany's financial success can be attributed to its productive economy, skilled labour force and quality of life. Germany holds a competitive edge in global markets because its economy is based on technological advancement, which has supported the rise in its economy (Ahmad et al., 101817).

Since the 1970s, Germany has constantly been at the forefront of research in Electrical Engineering, computer science and automotive engineering. Automotive engineering is one of Germany's most powerful industries. German engineers and scientists continue to create some of the most advanced automotive designs, such as semi-automatic gears, anti-lock braking systems (ABS) and airbags. Even though Germany is a relatively small country in terms of population, they have one of the highest numbers of researchers in electrical engineering and computer science (Udi et al., 10556). Several companies in Germany continue to manufacture advanced technologies that are being used by other countries.

Using innovative and high-tech products such as computers can help increase firms' productivity and competitiveness. This is beneficial for the economy as increased productivity leads to increased growth. In Germany, the use of advanced technologies contributed to the expansion of its economy.

In addition, Germany achieved high growth rates even though they were experiencing affordability problems and had difficulties catching up with other economies due to low levels of investment (Udi et al., 10561). Their advantage was that they were very competitive by keeping their wages down and maintaining a high degree of flexibility in their labour market through widespread segmentation and outsourcing.

Natural Resources

Earthy origin plays a significant part in economic growth in Germany. Natural resources support the development of Germany by enhancing its economy and contributing to high output and productivity. Germany's mineral deposits, soils, forests, water, inland waterways and coastlines are essential sources of natural resources (Balsalobre et al., 357).

Before 1990, the GDR had relied on extensive imports of raw materials; it was one of the global ten biggest importers of grain, the third-largest coal importer, and the fourth biggest importer of fertilizers. Natural resources also play a significant role in Germany's exports. For example, resource-based commercial enterprise such as iron and steel, chemicals and mechanical engineering are the most critical sectors of Germany's economy.

In addition, coal and lignite extractions in the Ruhr region have been significant natural resources contributing to their economic growth. Resource-rich countries are more likely to be self-sufficient and have higher per capita incomes than resource-poor countries (Fritsch and Wyrwich, 170). This benefits the economy as natural resources help produce high output and productivity.

Germany's rapidly growing economy was an example for other countries, and in return, other countries have taken steps to protect the environment and reduce pollution simultaneously. In conclusion, Germany has a wide variety of natural resources that play a role in the growth of its economy.

Physical Capital

Physical capital is a financial asset used to generate output and productivity in an economy (Bontis et al., 1373). According to the report, Germany's economic success can be attributed to its productive economy, skilled labour force and quality of life.

Germany has invested heavily in physical capital as they have invested heavily towards improving infrastructure such as roads, railways, ports, and airports, which have helped improve their economy. Physical capital increases productivity because it helps improve efficiency in the production of goods (Yu, 364). Physical money is divided into three in Germany's economy. These are Primary, secondary, and services.

Primary

Only 0.9 per cent of Germany's GDP in 2010 came from agriculture, forestry, and mining, which also employed only 2.4 per cent of the country's workforce, down from 4 per cent in

1991(Brenke, 22. Germany's agriculture is improbably prolific, and domestic production can encounter 90% of its nutritional request. After France and Italy, Germany is the third-largest agricultural producer in the European Union. Germany's top agricultural exports are potatoes, wheat, barley, sugar beets, citrus, and cabbage.

Secondary

Germany's secondary sector accounted for 14.4 per cent of the country's GDP in 2010 (Hoffmann and Lemieux, 132). This sector includes manufacturing, construction, and wholesaling, retailing and financial services. Germany has a solid industrial base and is a leading manufacturer of machine tools, precision equipment like electrical measuring equipment and scientific research instruments. It is also a leading exporter of consumer goods like sports goods and toys; pharmaceuticals, agricultural products and chemicals; textiles; plastics; chemical products; and engineering services for land vehicles.

Service

In Germany assistance sector contributes up to 70% of the entire GDP annually, while 72% of the employed people work in the service sector (Dustmann et al., 167). Since the start of the 19th century, there has been a noticeable growth in the service sector, caused by the high demand for people to work. In this sector, it embraces all businesses that deal with intangible things. These include services such as transport, hospitality and retailing. The service sector made up about 77% of all German employment in 2009, with 35% of all jobs in manufacturing. Germany also participates in cross-Border trade, which is especially important for the German economy.

Germany's economy has thrived in its physical capital and service sectors since the 1970s (Leamer and Store, 84). In fact, since the 1970s, Germany has change state to one of the quickest growing economies while maintaining a high level of exports. They achieved this by investing in physical capital and service sectors, and their economy has expanded its exports since that time.

Human Capital

The human capital account indicates the value of an individual's economic output combined with a measure of how productive they are in the economy (Teixeira and Queirós, 1642). Germany's human capital is high compared to other European countries. Over half of German citizens have completed tertiary education. In Germany, the percentage of young people with bachelor's degrees who are part of the workforce is increasing, and this is due to the overall high number of universities. This increases their productivity because they are more skilled and knowledgeable than others.

There has been a decrease in health care costs per capita as Germany's economy has grown (Prante et al., 148). This shows that with Human high capital, Germany can afford health care for their citizens and has been successful in terms of human capital.

Research Questions

1. What were Germany's economic growth steps in the last 50 years?
2. What policies were implemented, and how did they contribute to the economic growth of Germany?
3. How did the reforms form enabled economic growth in Germany?
4. How did the German model contribute to economic growth?

Research Objectives

General objectives

1. To analyze the economic growth of Germany over the last 50 years

Specific Objectives

1. To summarize how different policies that were enacted aided in economic growth.
2. To analyze the reforms
3. To explain the German economic model

Literature review

This section will entail Germany's economic growth, policies, programs, implemented strategies, and the economic growth model.

Economic growth

Chow, 119, defined economic growth as the growth of people's actual income. It is attributed to an increment in the volume of goods and services produced by a country. It is achieved through an increase in the productivity of workers or labour. Another definition of economic growth by Rodrik, 23 is the increase in an economy's income level. Various factors that lead to economic growth are natural resources, physical capital, human resources, technological advancements, skilled labour force, favourable conditions of the environment and networks.

The German economy is highly developed in the social market. It is ranked as the country with the sizable national economic system in Europe, the fourth with the ample nominal GDP in the world, and the fifth by GDP (Schoper et al., 83). Accordant to International Monetary Fund (IMF), Germany's social science growth was intense due to the country's unique mix of factors. The International Monetary Fund (IMF) has stated that the German market economy is well developed compared to others and attributes its strength to the integration between its various industries. The Real Market Economy determines that the German economy is highly developed in the social market due to government support and regulation in economic activity.

Germany implemented economic policies between the 1970s and 1980s. This resulted in the first phase of economic growth. During this phase, they faced challenges like low levels of investment and macroeconomic instability. The economy was sluggish; unemployment was high while wages remained stagnant. The government implemented policies that led to economic growth after stagnation. These policies included coordination of planning, enterprise and trade unions, and a flexible pricing system. Regionalization of industrial production was also implemented. The government also controlled the national steel sector and decided to run it as a monopoly. This helped stabilize the national output demand. This second phase of economic growth resulted in income per capita, a reduction in unemployment rates, a rise in export and investments and an increase in wages.

According to Belke, Dobnik and Dreger, 786 Germany's economy grew in the 1970s due to high energy consumption, a function of productivity. They used statistical analysis to conclude that consumption and production growth were positively correlated in the short run. Energy consumption impacted economic growth through its relationship with labour productivity.

Jaeger, 775, suggests that Germany's economy grew slowly during the economic recession from 2003 to 2010 because the country depended on foreign trade for growth. According to him, other factors aside from energy consumption were negatively correlated with change in Germany's economy and thus adversely affected its performance throughout the recession.

Germany experienced the third phase of economic growth. This was achieved with the implementation of the policies that were set by the government in the 1970s and 1980s, according to

Kuznets (33). The government implemented policies like regionalizing industrial production, a flexible pricing system, and solidarity from firms and trade unions regarding wages and costs. During this period, they faced low investment and macroeconomic instability challenges. However, they met other challenges like increasing levels of unemployment. Investments were low; thus economic growth rate was quiet, and the unemployment rate was increasing.

The economy grew at a high rate of 5 per cent. However, this would remain an exception since they are now going through a slow economic growth phase compared to what they experienced from 1991 to 2000. Inflation has also been rising during this period and was as high as 3.4 per cent in 1994. They have been experiencing a growth in trade during this period which has accumulated from 27 per cent to 40 per cent (Kindleberger, 2013). In addition, the production of export increased over time. In 1900, new industrialization was noted where Germany surpassed the United States and Britain in steel production. This is what was known as the growth of trade. From 1900 onwards, Germany has seen a lot of change in terms of business, leading to economic growth. This led to a financial miracle in 1913 caused by an unexpected population rise from a 35million to 67 million.

Bracke et al., 1154 claimed that 1990s, Germany saw a lot of foreign companies investing in their country, which boosted the economy and has been growing for decades even after World War 2. In 2000, the German economy experienced its first recession since 1945 and persisted until 2003. This was attributed to the euro's appreciation after 2002. During this period, Germany's economy stagnated. In 2008, the USA had an economic crisis, which was later imported to Germany. This dramatically decreased GDP in the fourth quarter of 2008 (Storm & Naastepad, 50).

The decline was still seen in 2009, but around mid-2009, Germany recovered in some sectors (Dribbusch et al., 218). Even though there was some recovery in 2009, the GDP still dropped by 4.7 per cent. The export-oriented sectors caused the decline, and the private consumption in the private sector was less affected. On the other hand, there was an economic recovery, and the annual GDP was 11.5 per cent. In 2011 Germany's economy was said to be at its peak. The German industries exported goods worth $1tillion, the advanced illustration in history. Also this year, the figure of employed people rose to 41.6. Still, the highest number recorded. In 2015Germany economy was regarded to have the most robust rates since it grew by 1.7 per cent in four years. According to the Federal Statistics Office, this was impelled by husky crimp in both private and public consumption. In 2020 there was a contraction of the GDP rate by 5% since it was affected by Covid-19.

Policies

Policies are rules and regulations implemented by a government to promote economic growth (O'Brien and Li, 456). According to them, policies may be seen as a strategy for promoting economic growth. Public investment criteria is a book that discusses and establishes the criteria needed when planning for public investments, which are aimed at developmental goals and not just money maximization. This means that the government sets policies to ensure that the country's GDP grows faster than in other countries. These policies include tax, economics, budget, and labour.

Tax Policy

The increased taxes that the German government implemented in the 1970s led to increased economic growth. According to Akçay and Türel (186), "Import-substituting industrialization" is one of the policies that have led to economic growth in Germany since World War 2. The government implemented this policy, which also included a level playing field for all industries. The subdivision of the euro currency in 2002 has led to a decline in the Deutsche Mark and other currencies previously used by Germany (Feldstein, 105). This led to an increase in exports and a decrease in imports. This has been attributed to economic growth in Germany since it affected imports and exports positively. The tax policy in Germany lost steam in the 20s, which was caused by political factors as well as macroeconomics. The rise of conservatism and the establishment of the Republic resulted from the Treaty of Versailles, which led to increased nationalistic feelings by the public. This led to a decline in tax rates.

Labour market policy

According to Tyson (460), the implementation of policies in Germany has led to an increase in inflation and labour shortages and wage inflexibility, which have affected productivity very much, thus leading to a decline in the economic growth rate. The government has been implementing policies that aim at promoting economic growth. Friedman (33) explained that these policies have led to an increase in trade and investments and thus an increase in GDP.

Germany's foreign economic policy

This policy was created to support German firms in the 19th century. This was done to expand market shares and face increased competition from state such as the United States and Britain. They also wanted to develop their industries to compete with companies from other countries.

Germany was able to join the European Community (ECC), which helped them export their goods to other European countries without paying customs duties. This meant that the exporters did not have to pay customs duties. Germany also pursued a policy of import substitution in the 1960s, which led to economic growth in Germany since it could not rely on imports since all industries were nationalized. The government also nationalized enterprises and initiatives to be allocated to private firms but at a cost to the government (Kindleberger, 2013). Four principles guided these policies which are as follows:

1. The government should avoid any investment in industries of little value that are not likely to be competitive with other industries worldwide.
2. The government should encourage enterprises to invest at home rather than abroad.
3. The government should support national firms over foreign firms by giving them cheaper resources and encouraging them to invest at home.
4. The government should develop new industries that could compete with imports

Programs

Agenda 2010

Programs are government policies that establish social science growth and improve the caliber of life of people in a country or a community (Neirotti et al., 27). The German government, which was at the time collaboration of Social Democrats and Greens, planned and carried out a series of changes known as Agenda 2010 to improve the country's welfare system and labour relations. Bruff (415) explained that Agenda 2010's goal was to encourage economic growth, which would lower unemployment. According to the OECD, Agenda 2010 was a series of reforms aimed at improving Germany's welfare system and labour relations (Dullien, 170). Following its implementation, several changes included decreasing unemployment from an average of 11.8% before its performance to 6.3% in 2011. The European Union member states are subjected to many rules and regulations by the Economic and Social Committee, which was formed in 1961. However, Germany was one of the first countries in Europe that were allowed to join the club. Germany is also one of the few countries with an economic growth rate higher than 4% (Möller, 166).

Belt tightening Reforms

Cost-cutting and job losses are not just happening in Europe's debt-ridden periphery anymore. To regain competitiveness as the eurozone enters its next downturn, several businesses in Germany, the currency bloc's largest economy, are likewise tightening their belts (Engelen, 54). Recent surveys indicate that the German economy is being held back by its weakening currency. The so-called "Deutsche Mark crisis" is one addition to a host of other problems in Europe's largest economy, which is dealing with an increasingly gloomy outlook for exports, high unemployment and large budget deficits. Germany's thriftiness expanded 0.2% in the second quarter, marking its worst performance since the third quarter of 2009, a quarterly drop that was less severe than expected. And unlike many other countries, Germany outperformed its neighbors in the eurozone. Additionally, it improved on the 0.5% decline this year's beginning.

Labor market reforms or Hartzz I- IV

Krebs and Scheffel 688 explained that after reunification with East Germany, the government implemented several policies to increase employment, especially for workers from the East. The reforms were aimed at reducing unemployment and increasing job creation. The first reform was called Hartz I, which reformed unemployment insurance, providing subsidies to companies that hire new employees. The second reform draft was known as Hartz II, which reformed the social welfare system and incentivized companies to hire more people who are considered long-term unemployed (Krebs and Scheffel, 699)

The third reform draft was known as Hartz III, which aimed to reform the labour market structure. This involved a shift of the cost burden to employees. The fourth reform involved the formation of Germany's first minimum wage set at 8.50 euros an hour which was supposed to be implemented in January 2015 but was delayed until 2017. This is mainly due to strong resistance from employers and unions who cannot agree on the extent of future exemptions to apply for the low-wage earner

(Bradley and Kügler, 124)

German model

The German model comprised an initial response to the crisis in the 1930s and the imperatives of post-war reconstruction (Fabre, 37). Thelen (154) explained that rejecting state intervention, Keynesian as in the USA and the U.K.K, and Colbertist according to the French model, the most critical aspect of the German model is the protection of fair and ordered competition. The state and the system of private property, which is based on the worker's right to work and relation of the effectuation of production, are legitimate in Germany (Lehndorff, 166). The fact that workers' rights are protected by law, alongside the activity of private property, seems to be a source of strength for the German economy in times of crisis. Germany has also overcome its most severe economic problem without inflation and state intervention in competition.

However, the German model is not immune to shocks. The main problem is demographic: Germany's growth model relies on an influx of young people into the workforce, and more recently; this growth pattern has been disrupted by a reduction in immigration from other European countries (Möller, 167).

Michel Albert [1] identified the core characteristics of the two "liberal" models of economic policy in a book published in 1991(Garrone, 145). Almost two decades later, the two models' comparison is still relevant for various reasons connected to their conflict with the two centuries of extensive globalization. Due to the challenge created by the compatibility and efficacy of the economic models used by its multiple participants, the issue is twice as important in France as it is in most eurozone countries. The 17 member states of the eurozone came up with a plan to end the crisis after two years of turmoil, including the concurrent growth of increased financial solidarity and tighter integration of budgetary policy.

As a result of its freedom from all forms of external restraint, the German policy, in contrast, is primarily based on the rejection of economic dependence on the capital markets. Germany, an obvious winner from opening the world's economies, appears to be laying out the winning recipe to benefit from globalization while improving its social security program and keeping its unemployment levels low. Germany has an external balance of about 4% of GDP. On the other hand, the United States and Japan run deficits of about 5% and 10%, respectively (Garrone, 144).

In the German model, the state is a guarantor of security and not an actual participant in economic activity. The renewal of social consensus is at the heart of this model. In contrast to France, citizenship means working for the state or a public or private organization or even being retired to earn privileges for life. In Germany, it means protecting personal property through laws universally respected by all parties to any transaction (Borrass et al., 21).

Summary

Various studies were conducted on the growth of Germany's economy after the crisis. There are a lot of explanations proposed by economists and experts regarding the growth and development of the German economy after the crisis. One focus is mainly on the labour market reforms and Hartz I-V, namely the Hartz IV merger program.

German labour market reforms are well known to be an essential aspect of the economic growth in Germany, and these policies played a important role in the past devolution of the German economy. In this regard, scholars interpret that it is right to say that Hartz IV reforms were essential for the existence of Germany's economy after the 2007-2008 global financial crisis.

There is a gap in the existing knowledge on the growth for the last 50 years because the research focuses on the causes of change in Germany before or after the crisis. But there is limited research on whether or not the reforms affected Germany's economic growth. However, this research will cover the gap through the collection of data and analysis, which will be handled in the next chapter.

ABSTRACT

Germany has been a prosperous nation for many years. The country managed to become economically independent and self-sufficient due to its strong financial sector, innovative technology, automobile, and efficient agricultural sectors. It is a world leader in science and engineering and has an impressive record of achievements in these sectors. It was one of the first nations to use industrial robots in the 1970s and 1980s. It has the highest share of patents per capita in Europe and the fourth-highest in the world.

It is a leading technology exporter, especially in computer hardware and software. The country's well-developed financial sector produced a surplus of 11 billion euros or 2% of national income. Germany's economy has grown steadily since unification, despite a slowdown in 2000-2003. Real GDP grew an average of 2.35% in the 30 years before confederation and 1.63% in the 30 years post-unification. From 1970-2007 real GDP growth was 1.04%, and from 2008-2012, it grew an average of 0.8%. Real GDP per capita rose from $28,000 in 1970 to $41,000 in 2010, a more significant increase than the U.S. Since 2005 Germany has been near full employment with just under 4% unemployment. The current account surplus stands at 7% of GDP, and the government budget exceeded 0.6% of GDP.

In this paper, we will explore how Germany achieved economic growth in the past 50 years by looking at various economic policies, programs, and strategic implementations that have contributed to this growing trend. The data was collected using secondary data and analyzed using Excel software.

CHAPTER 6
German Economy: Research Methodology

Data collection

The data will be collected using secondary sources. Sources include historical and current information on the economy of Germany. In secondary sources, we will find answers to the following questions:

The data collection begins with an extensive literature review of secondary sources, books and journal articles to understand what growth policies have worked in the past, why they worked, and how they contributed to Germany's economic growth. The impact on the German economy of any reforms introduced since 1991 is also to be highlighted.

Data analysis

The data will be accessed through Excel spreadsheets and Statistical Analysis Software (SAS). The Excel spreadsheets will be used to collect the data, view it, and analyze the various sources. The statistical analysis software will be used to see what component have add to Germany's economic development, assess the happening of different policies, and see how they have been implemented in the past and currently.

Limitations

The limitation of this project is data availability. All data will be collected by reading secondary sources. However, we might have to rely on one or two secondary sources if they contain the necessary information.

The statistical analysis software will have a limitation to see what happened in the past and how dividing Germany into East and West Germany has contributed to Germany's growth during the past 50 years since reunification.

CHAPTER 7
German Economy: Results and Findings

Exports

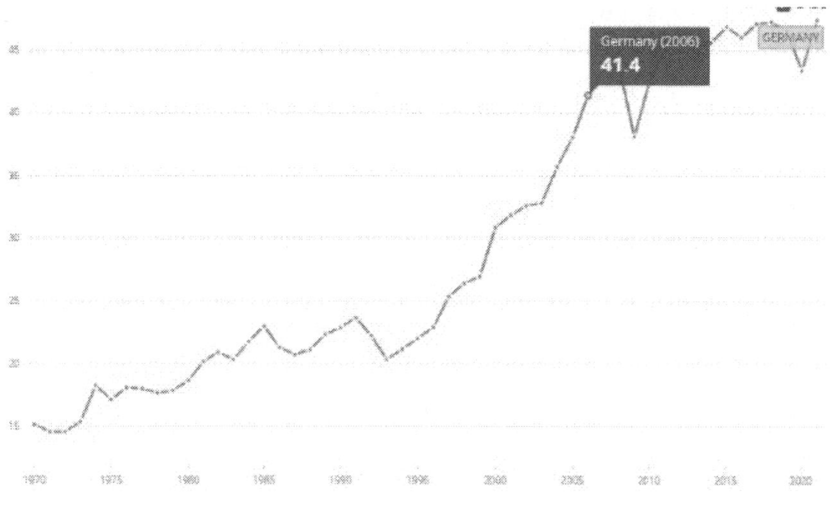

Figure 1: The average annual exports

As shown in figure 1, German exports have grown during the study period with a compound annual growth rate (CAGR) of three per cent and an increase of six per cent since 1990. This improvement in export growth has been driven by the rise in demand across all sectors but especially those associated with recent structural changes, such as electronics and chemicals, construction materials and machinery.

A section was also dedicated to foreign direct investments (FDI) into Germany, reflecting the country's economic performance, productivity and attractiveness as an investment destination. It would be essential to compare the FDI trends with those of exports. FDI into Germany increased by a CAGR of seven per cent during the study period but fell slightly since 1990. There has been a rock-steady rise in German exports from the 1990s to 2007. This was led by a mix of technological change and policy reforms enacted by the government.

In 2009 there was a fall in exports due to the global financial crisis. It can be said that German exporters were more resilient than those in the U.S.S and U.K.K, two major export markets of Germany. This was from $1640 billion (48.3%) in 2008 to $1300 (38.4% of GDP) billion in 2009.

The drop in exports did not result in a decline in production but led to the development of new products with higher value-added than previous ones. This has resulted in less pressure on real wages compared to other major exporting countries.

Then there was a notable rise in export between 2010 and 2015. The main reason for this increase in exports was the significant recovery experienced by the global economy. Exports to peripheral economies also saw a rise in demand.

In 2015 there was also a fall in exports from $ 1774.16 Billion in 2014 to $ 1575.40 billion in 2015. This was caused by the drop of dollar value in international trade due to strong fluctuations in prices and the exchange rates of commodities. In 2020 there was a steep fall from $ 1812.90 billion (46.62%) in 2019 to $1669.99 billion (43.42%). The COVID-19 outbreak caused this. This sharp export fall was experienced in 2009 after the 2008 financial crisis.

GDP

From authors

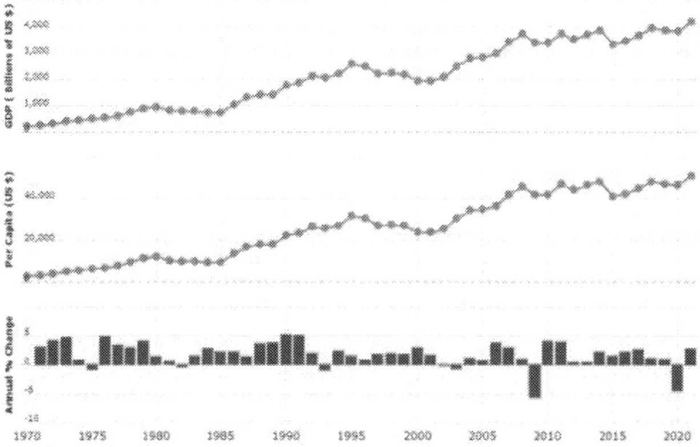

Figure 2: The GDP rating from 1970-2020

In 2020 was, the GDP in Germany recorded, and in 1970 was the lowest in 50 years. The estimated average is 2095.85 USD Billion from 1990 50 2020, signifying that there has been an increase in GDP. There was a slight fall in GDP in 1975 by -0.84 % from 1975 to 1980. This was due to the 2nd oil crisis. In the late 1970s, Germany experienced slow economic growth and rising unemployment. In 1980, West Germany's GDP per capita reached $11,868, exceeding that of all other European countries except France.

This was during the Cold War. West Germany subsequently enjoyed an economic upswing. In the 1970s and 1980s, growth was close to 4%. Year-on-year inflation remained lower than 3%.

In the early 1990s, Germany's GDP stagnated below 2%, threatening the stability of its export-driven economy. The labour market became increasingly weak, with unemployment rising to more than 11% of all workers by 1993. This led to a "squeeze" in Germany's economy as high inflation, although low by international standards, led to growing cost pressures that reduced margins for German exports and imports.

In the 1980s, Germany's crisis was triggered by the rise of corporate power. However, the German economy's robust performance in the early 1990s was due above all to governmental reforms (see below) and import substitution. In the early 1980s, Germany re-emerged as an economic superpower.

In 2002 and 2003, there was a contraction in GDP due to the poor performance of German exports and FDI (Foreign Direct Investments). Economist claimed that that was the worse stagnation Germany have ever experienced. In the last half of 2003, there was a weak recovery but was hardly noticed since it was a sustained revival. This led to a bloated welfare system, a rigid labour market, and chronically high unemployment. After 2004 there was a steady increase of 3.2% from 2005 to 2008 as the government tried to recover from the stagnation experienced in 2002 and 2003.

After the 2008 crisis, there was a downfall in GDP in 2009. According to the economist, this is the highest downfall ever in German GDP. There was a reduction in GDP from $3745.26 Billion (0.90%, $ 45613 per capita) in 2008 to $ 34 11.26 billion(-5.69%. $41650) per capita in 2009. The savings of the middle class and salaried workers were substantially diminished as a result of the reduction of the German medium of exchange. Due to the decreased spending power of the population throughout this economic downturn in Germany, small company owners and merchants suffered.

Then there was a slight recovery in 2010 of 1.3%, and in 2011 there was an increase of 4.0%. In 2012, Germany's GDP stood at an all-time high with a growth rate of 3.1%, surpassing the growth rate of all the other E.U.U countries combined by 0.8 per cent, which is significant considering that Germany is the 3rd big economy in the European Union behind France and Italy.

In 2014, Germany's GDP stood at an all-time high with a maturation rate of 2.1%. However, in the last quartern of 2014, the GDP contracted by 0.2%. Germany had not seen such a contraction in 7 years. This decrease was caused by the rising prices for oil and other commodities, which increased companies' production costs. Such costs were passed on to consumers, which decreased consumer spending and overall demand for goods and services throughout the German economy.

The German economy recorded a decline in GDP of -1.8% in 2015, the first decline since 2009, which shows a new trend of deflation. In 2016 Germany's GDP registered an increase of 0.7%. The European refugee crisis caused this. The weak performance of the German economy is caused by the high unemployment and a low growth rate for its exports.

In 2016 Germany's GDP stood at an all-time high with a growth rate of 1.9%. Germany's exports and private consumption caused this. In 2017 GDP increased by 1.7%. The last year had a positive

GDP growth rate in Germany. GDP growth rate declined from 1.9% in 2016 to -0.9% in 2017. Weak exports and investment caused this.

In 2018 there was stagnation in GDP. This was caused by the blame game relationship between Germany and the U.SS. The German government has been blaming the United States for their economic issues. In September 2018, Germany's exports to the U.S... Fell by 4 per cent from a year ago and were down 8 per cent annually using year-to-date figures. Over the previous three months, exports had fallen 14 per cent annually, according to data released by Destatis (German federal statistics office).

In 2020 also, there was a fall in the GDP by -4.57 % of the annual rate. This was caused by the outbreak of COVID-19, which led to a lockdown in the country. This hit hard the consumption sector and house holdings.

Population

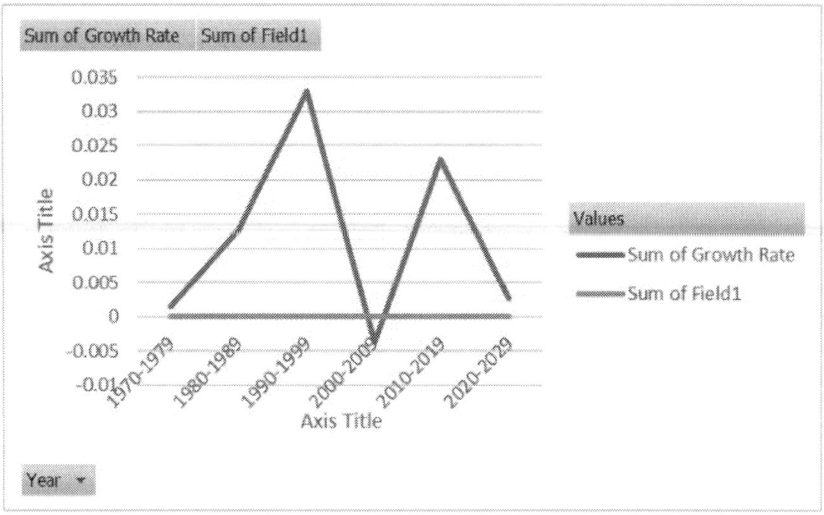

Figure 3: population growth in Germany

When calculating the growth of a country's economy, GDP is one factor to consider. Regarding the demographic future, net migration has impacted population development in the past decades. The state aims at a balanced development between historical population density and inner city overpopulation. Like other leading industrialized countries, Germany has to deal with the negative consequences of a decreasing fertility rate and an increased life expectancy of more than 80 years.

In the 1970s, West Germany had the lowest birthrate in Europe. In response, the government implemented several family incentives, including child allowances and tax breaks. However, these measures led to a temporary boost in births and increased deliveries by immigrant women. In the early 1980s, there was an increase in population due to economic reconstruction and communication technology advancement. This increased Germany's population growth rate to 0.4% in the 1980s, which resulted in a population of 80 million. This increase was also a result of increased urbanization.

During the post-unification period, the population of West Germany dropped and reached its lowest point in the early 1990s. This was due to a decline in fertility, which had been increasing steadily since the 1950s and more recently due to an increase in mortality rates, led by ageing and alcoholism. The East German population increased by 0.1% annually until 1990. Due to significant economic migration from East Germany to West Germany in the early 90s, population growth increased due to immigration.

The demographic increase rate between 1991 and 2016 was 0.8%, resulting in a population of 82 million and contributing to density declines in rural areas. During this period, the birthrate decreased due to record low fertility rates. This led to an average of 1.4 children per woman, which resulted in a decline in the grouping maturation rate to 0.

In the year 2000, it was reported that the German population grew by 1% to 82 million; this increase was due to the rise in life expectancy from 75 years to 83 years, high female employment and increased immigration. Since 2003, Germany's population has decreased, and 81.7 million people live there. The cause is that more individuals are passing away and dying faster than are giving birth. In 2005 it was revealed that Germany had the lowest birthrate since reunification. In 2006, the total fertility rate had reached 1.4 children per woman after remaining at a steady level of 1.

In 2010 there was a decrease in population growth. The reason for the decline was that no census had taken place in the last 30 years. The population growth rate in 2010 was 0.7% compared to 0.8% in 2009. The decrease in the population growth rate was mainly due to low fertility and the increase in life expectancy by four months, which resulted in a decline in the total fertility rate to 1.3 children per woman

The three factors driving population growth - immigration, fertility, and average life expectancy - might all increase if Germany maintains its present economic growth rate over the coming decades, and the population would essentially stay the same. GDP and population are two important economic factors, if they grow stronger together; they can lead to their economy's prosperity which results in high employment and low unemployment rate, so these two variables are very important for an economy.

Unemployment Rates

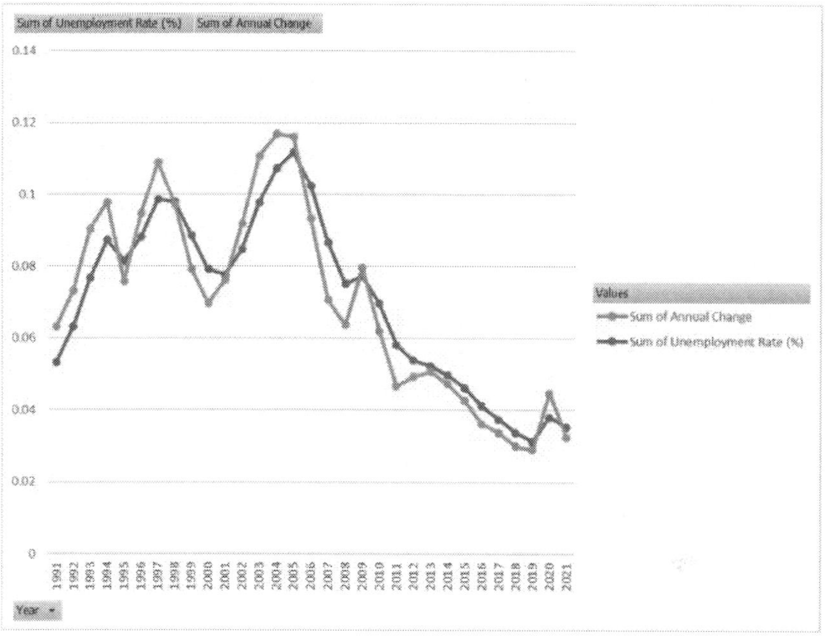

Figure 4; Unemployment rates from 1991-2021

The decrement in the GDP is reflected in the diminution in the pace of occupation; GDP and unemployment rates frequently go hand in hand. A hike in employment goes logically from higher GDP levels brought on by improving consumer request for products and services. The unemployment rate in German has reduced over time; there is broad agreement that structural factors such as broad factual wage costs to business organization, a lack of wage distinction, and escalating counterpart issues are mostly to blame for Germany's escalating unemployment rate in the 1990s. The unemployment rates of the 1950s and 1960s were high, but these high unemployment rates were attributed to unfavorable economic conditions.

After Germany's economy experienced high growth in the late 1980s, wages began to rise. Despite the large increase in unemployment due to unification, there was an overall decline in unemployment rates during the 1990s which resulted in low unemployment rates at the turn of the century. Germany's unemployment rate was 7.8% in 1994 and fell further to 6.2% in 1999. This reduction was due to economic growth, which resulted in fewer unemployed workers. At the same time, new job opportunities were created, and a small rise in women participating in the workforce.

In 2000, the unemployment rate had dropped from 10.4% in 1999 to 5.6%. However, the unemployment rate grew again in 2002 with the introduction of the euro. An increase in demand for skilled labour, and the labour shortage due to the large increase in school leavers who were trained for employment, caused a rise in unemployment. In 2006, it was reported that Germany's unemployment rate had reached 5.4% and was on track to exceed its pre-reunification level.

Since 2008 there has been a lessening in unemployment in the country. After the situation, there were labour market reforms made. In 2011, the unemployment rate decreased to 5.5%. By 2013, Germany's unemployment rate had increased to 6.6%.

Beginning in 2010, Germany's Unemployment Rate improved and reached a new record low. In 2017 the unemployment rate was at a record low level of 5.0%.

Germany's unemployment rate in 2020 was 4.2 per cent. Germany's unemployment rate steadily declined from 7.8% in 2019 to 4.2% in 2020. The low unemployment rate resulted from the German federal government's plan to invest in labour market policies and was due to Germany's economy gaining momentum in 2017 and 2018.

From authors

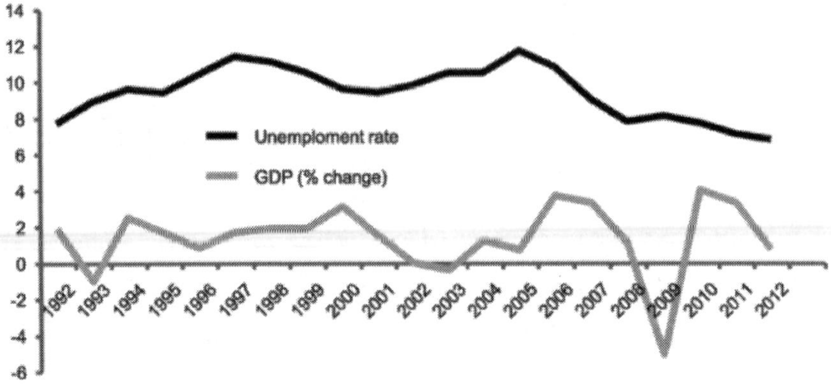

Figure 5: the relationship between unemployment rates and GDP from 1992- 2021.

The unemployment rate is the ratio between the unemployed and the population. The unemployment rate in Germany is higher than in other European countries. These countries try to decrease unemployment rates by training citizens for new jobs, thus reducing unemployment. Germany's policy also affects its unemployment rate because if an unemployed person receives a job in another country, it counts toward the total number of people employed and unemployed. Germany has a declining unemployment rate, and this makes the country's economy more stable. In the above diagram, the low unemployment rates lead to high GDP and economic growth. The relationship between unemployment and GDP is evident in Germany. The unemployment pace is the number of unemployed people in the working population. These two variables are relevant because a high level of unemployment is a significant problem for the country, so it's making its government try to get rid of it. In Germany, there are good employment opportunities, which helps decrease the unemployment rate. Besides that, Germany has an excellent educational system which makes people qualified enough to find jobs and have high standards of living. However, the unemployment rate could increase again if the economy does not grow as much as it should.

The German economy has grown rapidly over recent years, and the country's unemployment rate has declined since 2000. Over the long run, Germany's GDP and the unemployment rate have been correlated. German's economy is reflected in its unemployment rates, which have declined over time. Germany's unemployment rate was relatively high in the late 1980s and early 1990s. Unemployment rates subsequently declined over the remainder of the 1990s due to Germany experiencing a period of strong economic growth. This decline in the unemployment rate was attributed to increased employment opportunities and a rise in women participating in the workforce.

Summary and Conclusion

Summary

Germany is the quaternary largest economic system in the world. It is the leading country in Europe and a member of the G8. It is leading in innovations and the strong exports pillars. The component that have brought to the growth of Germany are unemployment rates, GDP rates, industrialization, and exports. Germany has a very high rate of social security and unemployment insurance. Despite being very strict in extending the benefits for unemployment insurance, on the contrary, Germany has not seen a rise in the unemployment rates. Germany is one of the directing countries in innovation, research and development. It got rid of its past stigma and is now known as a country that does not rely on imports for its exports. It has high educational levels, so it can attract highly skilled people from all over to provide them with better jobs. Germany is the 2nd largest exporter after China. It exports a lot to other countries, but Germany also imports. Around 50% of the exports are to be re-exported. Germany is committed to globalization and has high levels of productivity, human capital, and institutions.

Since 1970, Germany's economy has been increasing at an normal rate of about 3.25% for 30 years. The lowest point of the growth was between 1990 and 1993, due to reunification in Germany. This period was marked by negative growth and then a rebound after that. Since 1990, there has been a 1% decrease per year due to the reunification of East Germany.

The World Economic Forum (WEF) publishes the Global Competitiveness Index annually. In the 13-country eurozone, Germany's economy, which is the largest, grew by 2.5 per cent in 2006, the strongest rate of expansion since 2000. Germany has the strongest industrial sector in the eurozone. According to a WEF report, Germany was ranked third in terms of competitiveness. From 1995-2002, growth averaged 2.5% per year, which brought the economy to over $2 trillion in GDP. This growth is due to strong exports and investments. Although the recession continued into 2009, Germany made some progress toward recovery in the middle of the year. Despite a partial recovery in 2009, the GDP shrank by 4.7 per cent. Private consumer spending in the private sector was less impacted by the fall in export-oriented sectors. However, the economy was resurgent, and the annualized GDP was 11.5 per cent. At the end of 2011, a composite PMI indicated that manufacturing and services had begun to grow again and that the economy was starting to recover. The principal reason for this is the decline in price levels concerning foreign countries because they decided to introduce austerity measures. The European Central Bank tries to cut interest rates and encourage investment.

Germany has a highly developed labour market, which helps many sectors of its economy maintain high productivity levels. This has been achieved through investments in education, training, research, and development. Moreover, the country's social group security scheme provides a high plane of income protective covering and a high-quality pension system. In addition to the country's high overall productivity, Germany has achieved a high specialization in specific products and services. It is an industrial powerhouse with strong manufacturing and production industries and significant R&D investment.

Germany's trade balance reflects its position as one of the few countries that are both exporters and importers at very high levels. In 2018, leading exports were: machinery and transportation equipment, chemicals, vehicles and vehicle parts, plastics and rubber. Leading imports were: machinery and transportation equipment, chemicals, crude oil, and precious metals.

Germany has the world's ample manufacturing sector in footing of turnover (25% of global) and employees (18.6 million). Germany is the third-largest exporter in the world after China and theU.SS.

Tax Policies, Germany's corporate tax rates are very low. For example, in 2017, the corporate tax rate in Germany was 12.50%, lower than most countries and OECD member countries in general. In 2018, the federal and state governments agreed to reduce the overall German corporate tax rate by 33% over three years to 24%. Individual income taxes are also relatively low at almost 50% of GDP (compared to the OECD average of 37%).

Labour Market Policies. Germany's labour market has been reformed to create a flexible labour market that aligns with productivity needs. In the early 2000s, Germany implemented the so-called dual vocational system. This system provides many jobs and career opportunities for university graduates with vocational training and experience combined to make work more attractive. The federal government has played a key function in this reform, while the individual states have adopted different policies.

Germany's Foreign Economic Policy. In 2000, the German government introduced a new foreign trade policy that took into account environmental and social concerns, as well as the interests of trade partners. The new trade policy advanced market-opening measures to promote sustainable development overseas. This is a significant shift from the traditional focus on Germany's competitiveness alone. It also shows how Germany's economic policy is guided by its reform strategy, globalization, and the goals of its social market economy.

The reforms that have been adopted in Germany have helped to increase its economic growth. These reforms were Agenda 2010, belt-tightening, and Hartz-IV. The first reform agenda was implemented in 2003. This agenda focused on the economy's growth through tax cuts, investment incentives, and a reduction in welfare benefits. Plan 2010 was meant to reduce the influence of bureaucracy on organization and business decisions. The Hartz IV reform was introduced in 2004 and was meant to incentivize employment through lower income taxes further. Chancellor Merkel initiated the belt-tightening reform in 2008, but it is still ongoing until now. Some of the policies that were imposed on government expenditure and social services included austerity measures.

The Agenda 2010 reform has been meant to tackle the dual labour market problems of low employment, low wages, and high welfare spending. It is designed to produce higher and lower unemployment rates through reforms that promote growth, especially in small and medium enterprises (SMEs). Furthermore, it was designed to reduce bureaucracy in business decisions. There was a reduction in corporate tax rates from approximately 48% to 30%. Belt-tightening measures have been implemented to reduce welfare spending and increase competitiveness in the labour market. The reform in Germany has contributed to economic growth. The main factor contributing to the reform is the low unemployment rate and high education rate of the labour force, which has attracted companies to invest in Germany. Another factor that also played a big role in its economic growth is that it started a transfer payment program for people with disability and that above retirement age. This transfer program will help many unemployed people willing to work but could not find jobs.

The model of Germany is called the social market economy, and this model has contributed to the economic growth in Germany. The social market economy combines the principles of liberal economic, corporatist social, and democratic polity. The principles deeply rooted in German society helped Germany achieve economic growth. The German economy follows the principles of "Liberating Market Concepts" and "Liberalization." Germany's policies have contributed to productivity growth, job creation and good employment opportunities. The other model adopted by Germany is the dual vocational training system. This model allows students to earn a competitive wage by combining professional training with on-the-job experience. In addition,

Germany has also embraced globalization, which has helped its economy to grow globally.

Conclusion

Three main factors helped Germany to achieve the current economic maturation in terms of occupation creative activity, employment and productivity. The first factor is the social market economy that the Germans established. This model has been followed since the early 20th century, contributing to Germany's economic growth. The second factor is the state's active policies like Hartz IV, which helped to create more jobs and recruit more people into the industries. The third factor was its policies on infrastructure development and transportation.

Various challenges affect the economic growth of Germany and all European Union member countries. The main challenge of Germany is to overcome the dual labour market problems, which is why they focus on building more infrastructure and transportation systems in Germany.

Low Wage Growth and Inflation

Greece's economic troubles are having an impact on Germany and the other European countries. The overall economic situation in Germany, characterized by low wage growth coupled with inflation, is good for large companies that can afford to raise their prices and thus increase their profits. However, it is bad for smaller companies and employees affected by stagnant wages and limited job opportunities. Germany's economy has been hard hit due to the export industry and the country's higher skill level.

Crisis

The 2008 crisis was a challenge for Germany's economic growth. The economic growth of Germany has reduced by two percentage points in 2009 and one point in 2010. Germany is still recovering from the downturn, with unemployment remaining at its lowest level for nearly 20 years at 5.2%. Still, the current economic recovery may stall without a further expansion of credit for businesses and a firm commitment to structural reform. One weakness throughout the financial crisis has been the slower-than-expected pace of reduced unemployment, which means that wages haven't kept pace with price rises.

COVID-19 Pandemic

Since 2019, Germany has been chosen as the best performing OECD economy. As of 31st December 2018, the unemployment rate was 4.9%. The Gross Domestic Product (GDP) growth rate was 3.2% annually throughout 2018 and has been forecasted to reach 2.1% in 2019 and 1% in 2020.

Europe and Cross-Border Increased Risk

Germany's economy is highly exposed to the eurozone, and the country is vulnerable to shocks from that part of the world. Germany's biggest trading partner is the United States, and given the current economic recovery in that part of the world, Germany's economy will continue to grow. The possibility of a no-deal Brexit could also affect Germany's economic growth.

REFERENCES ON GERMANY

Janik, M., 2021. Economic and Political Reconstruction and Development of FRG after World War II. Historia i Polityka, 43(36), pp.139-151.

Scherner, J., Streb, J. and Tilly, S., 2014. Supplier networks in the German aircraft industry during World War II and their long-term effects on West Germany's automobile industry during the 'Wirtschaftswunder'. Business History, 56(6), pp.996-1020.

Gilpin, R.G., 2015. France in the Age of the Scientific State (Vol. 2046). Princeton University Press.

Dustmann, C., Fitzenberger, B., Schönberg, U. and Spitz-Oener, A., 2014. From sick man of Europe to economic superstar: Germany's resurgent economy. Journal of economic perspectives, 28(1), pp.167-88.

Ouoba, Y., 2020. Natural resources fund types and capital accumulation: A comparative analysis. Resources Policy, 66, p.101635.

Ragnitz, J., 2019. Thirty Years after the Berlin Wall Came Down: Economic Transition Completed, but Structural Deficit Remains. ifo DICE Report, 17(03), pp.22-27.

Ahmad, M., Jiang, P., Majeed, A., Umar, M., Khan, Z. and Muhammad, S., 2020. The dynamic impact of natural resources, technological innovations and economic growth on ecological footprint: an advanced panel data estimation. Resources Policy, 69, p.101817.

Udi, J., Bekun, F.V. and Adedoyin, F.F., 2020. Modeling the nexus between coal consumption, FDI inflow and economic expansion: does industrialization matter in South Africa?. Environmental Science and Pollution Research, 27(10), pp.10553-10564.

Balsalobre-Lorente, D., Shahbaz, M., Roubaud, D. and Farhani, S., 2018. How economic growth, renewable electricity and natural resources contribute to CO2 emissions?. Energy Policy, 113, pp.356-367.

Fritsch, M. and Wyrwich, M., 2017. The effect of entrepreneurship on economic development—an empirical analysis using regional entrepreneurship culture. Journal of Economic Geography, 17(1), pp.157-189.

Jaeger, C., 2011. The role of foreign trade in Germany's economic growth during the recession years 2003-2010: the potential for endogenous input-output linkages. Energy Economics, 33(5), pp.772-780.

Kuznets, S. 2019 Economic growth and income inequality. In The gap between rich and poor (pp. 25-37). Routledge.

Kindleberger, CP.., 2013. Europe's postwar growth. In Europe's Postwar Growth. Harvard University Press.

Bracke, T., Bussière, M., Fidora, M. and Straub, R., 2010. A Framework for Assessing Global Imbalances 1. The World Economy, 33(9), pp.1140-1174.

Storm, S. and Naastepad, C.W.M., 2016. Myths, mix-ups, and mishandlings: understanding the Eurozone crisis. International Journal of Political Economy, 45(1), pp.46-71.

Dribbusch, H., Lehndorff, S. and Schulten, T., 2017. Two worlds of unionism? German manufacturing and service unions since the Great Recession. Rough waters. European trade unions in a time of crises, Brussels, ETUI, pp.197-220.

Belke, A., Dobnik, F. and Dreger, C., 2011. Energy consumption and economic growth: New insights into the cointegration relationship. Energy Economics, 33(5), pp.782-789.

Chow, G.C., 2017. Capital formation and economic growth in China. In Chinese Economic History Since 1949 (pp. 1186-1221). Brill.

Rodrik, D. (2014). The past, present, and future of economic growth. Challenge, 57(3), 5-39.

Schoper, Y.G., Wald, A., Ingason, H.T. and Fridgeirsson, T.V., 2018. Projectification in Western economies: A comparative study of Germany, Norway and Iceland. International Journal of Project Management, 36(1), pp.71-82.

O'Brien, K.J. and Li, L., 2017. Selective policy implementation in rural China. In Critical Readings on the Communist Party of China (4 Vols. Set) (pp. 437-460).

Akçay, Ü. and Türel, O., 2022. Import-Substituting Industrialization Strategy and Planning Experience in Turkey, 1960–1980. Political Economy of Development in Turkey, pp.163-195.

Feldstein, M., 2012. The Failure of the Euro: The little currency that couldn't. Foreign Aff., 91, p.105.

Tyson, J., 2016. Shock watch Bulletin Sub-Saharan Africa's economic downturn and its impact on financial development. ODI Working Paper No 440.

Friedman, B.M., 2017. The moral consequences of economic growth. In Markets, morals & religion (pp. 29-42). Routledge.

Duell, N., Thurau, L. and Vetter, T., 2016. Long-term unemployment in the EU: Trends and policies (p. 12). Gütersloh: Bertelsmann Stiftung.

Neirotti, P., De Marco, A., Cagliano, A.C., Mangano, G. and Scorrano, F., 2014. Current trends in Smart City initiatives: Some stylized facts. Cities, 38, pp.25-36.

Bruff, I., 2010. Germany's Agenda 2010 reforms: Passive revolution at the crossroads. Capital & Class, 34(3), pp.409-428.

Dullien, S., 2014. German reforms as a blueprint for Europe?. In Competitiveness in the European Economy (pp. 162-176). Routledge.

Möller, J., 2018. The future of the German model after the labour market reforms. In A Global Perspective on the European Economic Crisis (pp. 162-178). Routledge.

Engelen, K.C., 2020. Germany on the Firing Line. The International Economy, 34(1), pp.50-66.

Krebs, T. and Scheffel, M., 2013. Macroeconomic evaluation of labor market reform in Germany. IMF Economic Review, 61(4), pp.664-701.

Bradley, J. and Kügler, A., 2019. Labor market reforms: An evaluation of the Hartz policies in Germany. European Economic Review, 113, pp.108-135.

Fabre, A., 2012. The German economic model: A strategy for Europe. Economic Issues, 37.

Thelen, K., 2000. Why German employers cannot bring themselves to dismantle the German model. Unions, employers, and central banks: Macroeconomic coordination and institutional change in social market economies, pp.138-172.

Lehndorff, S., 2015. Model or liability? The new career of the 'German model'. Divisive Integration: The triumph of failed ideas in Europe–Revisited, pp.149-178.

Möller, J., 2015. Did the German model survive the labor market reforms?. Journal for Labour Market Research, 48(2), pp.151-168.

Garrone, M., 2011. Prehospital ultrasound as the evolution of the Franco-German model of prehospital EMS. Critical Ultrasound Journal, 3(3), pp.141-147.

Borrass, L., Kleinschmit, D. and Winkel, G., 2017. The "German model" of integrative multifunctional forest management—Analyzing the emergence and political evolution of a forest management concept. Forest Policy and Economics, 77, pp.16-23.

Teixeira, A.A. and Queirós, A.S., 2016. Economic growth, human capital and structural change: A dynamic panel data analysis. Research Policy, 45(8), pp.1636-1648.

Prante, F.J., Bramucci, A. and Truger, A., 2020. Decades of tight fiscal policy have left the health care system in Italy ill-prepared to fight the COVID-19 outbreak. Intereconomics, 55(3), pp.147-152.

Leamer, E.E. and Storper, M., 2014. The economic geography of the internet age. In Location of international business activities (pp. 63-93). Palgrave Macmillan, London.

Dustmann, C., Fitzenberger, B., Schönberg, U. and Spitz-Oener, A., 2014. From sick man of Europe to economic superstar: Germany's resurgent economy. Journal of economic perspectives, 28(1), pp.167-88.

Hoffmann, F. and Lemieux, T., 2016. Unemployment in the Great Recession: a comparison of Germany, Canada, and the United States. Journal of Labor Economics, 34(S1), pp.S95-S139.

Brenke, K., 2014. Eastern Germany still playing economic catch-up. DIW Economic Bulletin, 4(11), pp.6-23.

Bontis, N., Janošević, S. and Dženopoljac, V., 2015. Intellectual capital in Serbia's hotel industry. International Journal of Contemporary Hospitality Management, 27(6), pp.1365-1384.

Yu, H., 2017. Motivation behind China's 'One Belt, One Road'initiatives and establishment of the Asian infrastructure investment bank. Journal of Contemporary China, 26(105), pp.353-368.

CHAPTER 8
Mitigating the risks of globalization through localization

Globalization

Sassen (2015) defined Globalization as the act of transferring products, services, and ideas across national borders, has the potential to have major impacts on a global scale. Such impacts are often beneficial for developing economies due to the increase in trade and production resulting from Globalization. Concern about Globalization and its effects on local markets has been rising for years. (Autio, Mudambi, and Yoo, 2021:3-16) also defined globalization is "the transfer of products, technology, and ideas from one part of the world to another, usually from developed to developing countries". Companies need to understand how their actions affect the market in which they operate. Through marketing research, companies can learn about their customers' purchasing practices, weighing products and services against one another (Passas, 2017).

Globalization according to Baylis, 2020, it has its weakness and strengths. He claimed that it affects countries differently depending on how strong their economy and political environment is. However, there can be negative impacts on those unable to compete with established companies in developed countries because of increased competition for similar jobs or small industries trying to sell their goods internationally. The world has become less localized with the advent of Globalization (Wang and Sun, 2021).

The historical aspect of Globalization

Amartya Sen, an economist who won the Nobel Prize, asserts that globalization has always evolved and that the geographical discoveries of the sixteenth century and the discovery of America in 1492 led to a similar type of globalization with an advanced civilization (Ershov et al., 2019). In terms of relevance and degree of engagement in various nations worldwide, phenomena comparable to the process of globalization have been observed throughout the history of this planet, even in long-gone eras. Mathematicians in the Arab world swiftly adopted the decimal system once it first arose in India between the second and sixth centuries AD. Following mathematics' introduction to Europe in the second part of the eleventh century, globalization once more followed (Burlacu et al., 2018).

Baylis, 2020 claimed that Globalization is not brand-new. Since the dawn of civilization, neighbors have been exchanging products. As cultures developed, they gained the ability to travel further to exchange their items for valuable ones obtained from other cultures. An early example of Globalization is the Silk Road, a web of historical trade routes that connected Europe, North Africa, East Africa, Central Asia, South Asia, and the Far East (Peters, 2021:955-961).

Although some academics, philosophers, and sociologists contend that the roots of globalization go back many centuries, Theodore Levitt, an American economist, is credited with coining the word (Hancock, 2021). Ever since the phrase has almost completely supplanted the commonly used phrase "global village." The overall liberalization of the market process was established, supervised by the GATT, and later by the WTO, IMF, and World Bank Investment. This transformation can be traced back to the G6 conference in Rambouillet (France) in 1975. Since then, various definitions of the phenomenon of globalization have been put forth. For instance, the ODCE describes it as "a process through which markets and production in different countries are becoming increasingly interdependent due to the dynamic exchange of goods and services and through movements of capital and technology (Zhang et al., 2022)."

Europeans traded Chinese silk and spices for glass and manufactured products for more than 1,500 years, helping to create a global economy in which both Europe and Asia were accustomed to imports (Hancock, 2021). Globalization took off after Europeans discovered the New World; the vast exchange of organisms, cuisines, civilizations, and ideas became known as the Columbian Exchange. Another illustration of Globalization is the Triangular Trade network, in which ships transported manufactured goods from Europe to Africa, enslaved people to the Americas, and raw materials back to Europe (SIDDIQUI, 2020). The rise of slavery, as a result, reveals how readily Globalization can harm people and link them.

Because of the quickening pace of communication and transportation improvements, Globalization has accelerated recently. Businesses can now find investment opportunities because of communication advancements (Thompson and Dahling, 2019:673). Information technology advancements allow for immediate communication and a quick transfer of financial assets across international borders. Globalization is also aided by improved domestic fiscal regulations and trade agreements among nations (Yaya, Otu, and Labonté, 2020:1-7). Globalization is also facilitated by political and economic stability. Experts point to one of the reasons why Africa has not profited from Globalization as much as countries in Asia and Latin America are the relative instability of many African governments. Globalization has begun affecting all aspects of human existence, including development and security. Several factors cause the effects of Globalization:

Technology - The rapid diffusion of information through the Internet, satellite TV, and cellular phones have decreased the cost and time involved in communication between nations (Oi, Fukuda, and Sako, 2020:52-65). As a result, information about developing markets can be quickly obtained, allowing developing countries to develop more quickly.

Empowerment - Technology has allowed global minimum wage and poverty issues to be more easily addressed (Thompson and Dahling, 2019:673).

Trade - Trade among countries has increased thanks to Globalization greatly. The average trade in goods between Europe and the United States has jumped by 2,000 percent since 1950(Klein, and Pettis, 2020).

Economic power - Recent economic events have shown that the world is becoming more economically powerful, meaning that fewer and fewer countries will be able to compete with wealthier nations (Ake, 2019:19-42).

Social impact - The Globalization of certain aspects of society (women's rights, religious freedom.) can negatively impact various communities worldwide that are unprepared for these changes (Roberts, 2019:114-131).

Global considerations

i. Market entry strategy: A foreign market can be penetrated in various ways, including exporting, licensing, franchising, collaborating, mergers and acquisitions, and general partnerships (Pegan et al., 2020:23-38).

ii. Global branding: The Globalization of branding has increased as businesses try to capitalize on the increasing number of global consumers. The global trend is focused on marketing at a regional level, rather than just locally or nationally. This has been driven by "macro-level" factors such as the need for globally consistent branding in a world with greatly differing political and cultural environments (Contractor et al., 2019:3-18). Many companies have international headquarters that control how product lines are branded (Branding control).

iii. Supply chain: In global supply chains, parts and components are often sourced from diverse suppliers and manufactured in many locations (Alexander, 2020:269-290). Global supply chains tend to employ different technologies than local ones, so companies should consider both the resource management needs of their global supply chain and their local maintenance needs.

iv. Regulations: Companies doing business across international borders need to understand the regulations of the countries they operate in. This can include local labor laws, taxes, licensing requirements, and social considerations such as race or gender orientation (Gaughan and Javalgi, 2018).

Risks involved with Globalization

Globalization has risks as well as rewards. The risks of Globalization are the things that can go wrong. Risks include:

I. Labor: Globalization has created underemployment, which means that people who want full-time jobs don't have them because they are forced to work part-time or temporary jobs. This is the most immediate threat to labor in developing countries, especially when high unemployment rates already exist. Another argument against Globalization can be made about its impacts on employment for workers in developed nations (O'Rourke,

2019:356-382). Increased competition in global markets has forced many industries to close or cut jobs. This contributes to the problem of unemployment, which is often present in developed nations.

II. Culture: Traditionally, culture was the primary social framework that bound people together. Throughout history, cultures have been at odds with each other, but with Globalization, these conflicts have become more frequent and severe (Kato et al., 2022:1113-129). Conflict over religious values, nationalism and cultural symbols are some causes of cultural conflict. A recent example is the Middle East crisis during the late 1990s. Increased global trade encourages cultural assimilation and causes constant cultural conflicts and tensions.

III. Globalization: The inescapable fact is that Globalization or Globalization has been upon us for years. In the UK, it is popular to criticize Globalization on a grander scale. Everyone should get used to it, and that's what the government seems to be doing with the latest report on why we have not seen a recession, according to the BBC News section of their website on 13th June 2012(Tight, 2021).

IV.Environmental: Different synthetic materials have been dumped into the ground as a result of Globalization and industrialization, which has led to the growth of many dangerous weeds and plants. By interfering with their genetic makeup, this toxic substance has caused a great deal of harm to plants. The available land resources have been constrained. Massive fruitless areas have been trampled over to make room for new construction. While some may rejoice in these technological advances now, they may have long-term effects on the climate. To lower manufacturing costs and boost competitiveness, enterprises give up adding costs to decrease environmental pollution into the price of the product. It causes environmental imbalance, climate change, and severe natural disasters. (He et al., 2019:155-166)

V. Inequality: As a result of outsourcing and an increase in the migration of foreign workers, Globalization manifests its most detrimental effects on inequality by leading to the loss of many employees (Van Barneveld et al., 2020). The number of competitive businesses also grows as a result of Globalization. Only the strongest businesses with the best technology thrive, which increases the wealth of the most successful businesses. The world's lowest half of the population is controlled by 388 persons, according to Oxfam reports from 2011. Compared to earlier, only 62 people now hold most of the wealth after five years (Young, 2018:241-251).

Beneficial and loser of Globalization

As said above Globalization favour or affects different countries differently. Below is a graph illustrating the same:

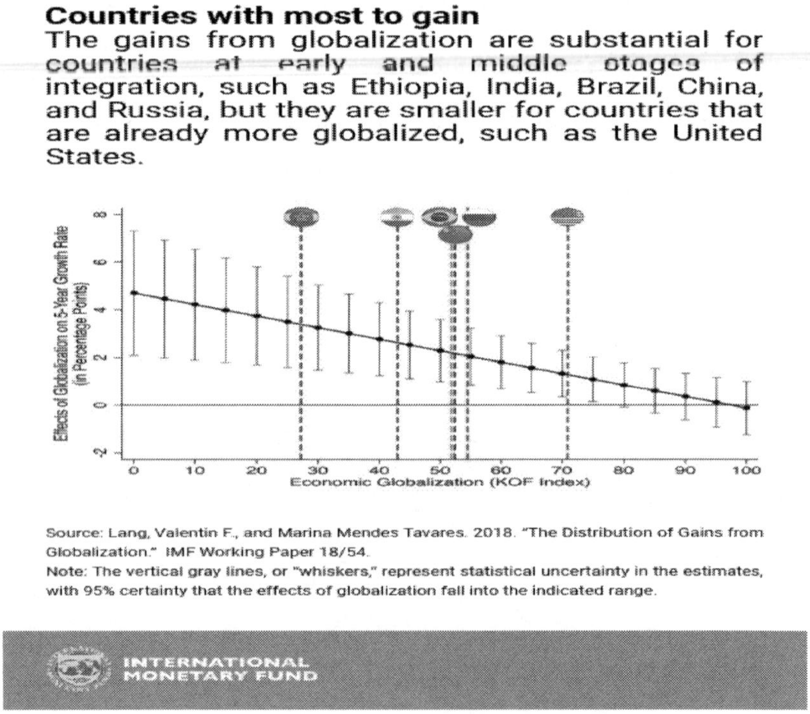

Figure 1: Beneficial of Globalization

The black line depicts the impact of a one-point rise in economic globalization on a country's five-year growth rate. Developing nations like Ethiopia, whose flag is displayed on the far left, stand to gain more than mature economies like the United States, whose flag is displayed on the far right. The graph also displays the degree of globalization and future growth prospects of nations like India, Brazil, China, and Russia.

His distribution of income increases among nations is also evaluated in the study by Rodrik (2018). It reveals that increased economic disparity, which occurs when more money goes into the wallets of the wealthy than the poor, is frequently linked to globalization. While globalization generally benefits both the affluent and the poor in developing nations, it frequently has little impact on the earnings of the poor in many industrialized economies (Keohane and Nye, 2020).

But to spread the benefits of globalization more widely, government actions are important (Ake, 2019). Globalization may achieve its goal of producing advantages for all through raising skill levels via investments in education and through taxes and transfers that spread the benefits more widely.

Localization

Adapting a piece of content's complete meaning for a target market through localization entails considering translation, related images, and cultural factors that affect how your message is interpreted (Konrad-Mangy and Takyi, 2018:17-24). The term "localization"According to Zafari Gkelias and Leung (2019) refers to the concentration of a certain industry in a given neighbourhood, location, or area. The geographical division of labour, or specialization by areas or regions, is connected to localization. A single town or area frequently specializes in the manufacture of a specific good. When localization is done correctly, a piece of content will be equally effective in its translation to as many languages as the target customers (Shafirova and Cassany, 2019).

Kundu (2014) claimed that without sufficient understanding, organization, and management of these factors, risk increases for all parties involved. Beyond translation, localization gives a product, website, or service the impression that it was created for a local audience by a local audience (Poppi, 2016). Businesses must modify their operations to fit each target market's cultural norms to implement a successful localization strategy.

The goal of localization explained by Aurambout et al. (2019:1-21) is to return the economy to a human scale. It is the process of creating economic institutions that enable the production of the goods and services required by a community to occur as often as feasible locally and regionally. As a result, there will be less pollution and environmental damage, improving human health and material well-being and strengthening communal cohesiveness.

Localization can also be defined through the International Organization for Standardization (ISO) as "the adaptation of text within one design and format to a particular cultural context," is a crucial part of communications between the developed and developing world explained by Dunne (2014). Mitigating the risks of globalization through localization is arguably the best solution to ensuring that globalized products and services are well received in their target markets (Bryson and Vanchan, 2020). Risk is inherent in any business enterprise, but risks can be reduced by identifying those that can negatively impact a project's success and then taking action to control them. Localizing a project during its design makes it possible to efficiently mitigate the risks of globalization, thus increasing its chances for success.

Benefits of localization

Improving environmental health:

Reducing the scale of economic activity is essential for slowing climate change and reversing ecological degradation. This doesn't mean our quality of life will also be reduced: place-based economies excel at promoting both human well-being and environmental health. For example, small-scale ecological farms produce more food per acre than industrial monocultures while supporting soil health and wildlife (Altieri and Nicholls, 2020).

Localizing our economies means minimizing climate-changing emissions while improving air, soil, and water quality.

Human communities can be healthy when they are small and densely populated. That's why many of the world's most livable cities are highly localized: Vancouver, Vienna, and San Francisco (James, 2014).

Localizing our economies also makes sense from a global point of view:

Cooperation is often more effective than competition; working together has allowed many people to live longer and better (Morschheuser et al., 2019:7-24). Localizing will help us shift our relationship with nature away from hubris, economic exploitation, and domination. Localization builds capacity for change in developed and developing countries by helping people become more self-reliant and resilient in the face of destabilizing processes such as climate change and globalization.

Increasing place-based jobs:

Increased place-based employment directly contributes to the health and prosperity of local communities. This employment would result from tighter regulation of multinational firms and banks and revitalizing neighborhood businesses and food systems (Bailey, 2012:1-35). Increased local employment would increase the total number of jobs in each community and provide more economic opportunities for people at all education and skill levels (Helyer and Lee, 2014). Localized economies will also likely have greater wage growth than non-localized economies, which can bring higher incomes to workers who are currently outside the worldwide labor market (Sinha, 2018).

Encouraging community cohesion:

"Community development lies at the heart of sustainable post-growth strategies."(Soper, 2020) Localization will strengthen the vital ties that bind communities together. Localization will also help communities strengthen their distinct identities and give them a greater chance to maintain their cultural integrity (Sasaki et al., 2019:793-831). Localization can avoid many social and economic problems that occur whenever people are thrown together from different cultural backgrounds (Sabaratnam, 2020).

Promoting authentic content:

Authentic communication between cultures requires time and effort. The localizing text requires more than simply translating words; it requires understanding the local context, culture, and values to craft words that come alive for all those who read them in their original language (Feder-Nadoff, 2022).

Reducing global poverty:

Localization will reduce global poverty. Local markets can support those without access to markets in the developed world because they can sell their products locally (Quayson et al., 2020).

Artisans and artists can create high-quality goods suited to local tastes and preferences using local resources and materials. In developed countries, locally produced goods (for example, honey from an apiary in Eilat) help promote healthy communities as they may incorporate different food groups than what people are used to eating at home or in the marketplace (McGenity et al., 2020). In addition, localization will help populations in developing countries become self-reliant and increase their capacity for social resilience. Choosing to be local is a choice that makes sense from a global perspective; choosing to remain global is a path filled with uncertain consequences.

Invigorating democracy:

Large firms lose influence due to localization, which also gives common people a stronger political voice (Bradford, 2020). Because it protects small-business owners' livelihoods while solving environmentalists' concerns, and because it can appeal to both free market republicans and progressive socialists, the localization movement has immense potential to help us overcome the entrenched Left/Right split.

Localization can help us break the stranglehold of economic globalization and open up more opportunities for democratic political action. Localized economies in developing countries also promote democracy by building domestic markets, which increases self-reliance and reduces international dependence (CHACKO, 2021). Localized economies will not be dominated by multinational corporations and banks but will strengthen the influence of small-scale businesses, local governments, and nongovernmental organizations (Zhu, 2019).

Promoting regional development:

Regional economics is geared towards helping communities thrive within a larger regional economy. The creation of regional economies will strengthen communities, improve environmental health, protect local jobs and create more egalitarian wealth distribution (Arndt et al., 2022:1-26). Localized economies can help cities and regions build a more robust manufacturing sector and provide greater supply chains for local goods so that people have more access to safe, affordable food. Localization will help people achieve a more equitable distribution of wealth and a healthier environment.

Reversing globalization:

The effects of globalization, such as the loss of cultural identity, increased inequality between and within nations, and the undermining of the human community, have all contributed to an increase in xenophobia, racism, and anti-Semitism (Casaglia et al., 2020). Localizing our economies will help reverse these destructive trends by supporting communities' cultural integrity and allowing people to interact on a smaller scale with those different from them.

Slowing urban sprawl:

Many individuals are under psychological, financial, and governmental pressure to relocate from rural to metropolitan areas (Rodríguez-Pose and Storper, 2020). The majority of people on Earth still reside in rural areas. Compared to their urban counterparts, these folks have a lesser ecological imprint and are more independent. A greater balance between the urban and rural areas results from localization, which promotes investment in place-based resources and jobs. Localizing economies will help reduce urban sprawl, strengthen communities and increase job opportunities in rural areas (Rodríguez-Pose and Storper, 2020). Urban sprawl often leads to the degradation of rural areas because urban growth consumes land once used by rural communities.

Removing barriers to fair trade:

Fairtrade can no longer be viewed as an alternative model but must be understood as a mainstream option from which all people have a right to benefit (Sahan, 2019:14-23). The World Trade Organization (WTO) may act as a disincentive for fair trade, but once the WTO rules on whether or not fair trade is legal are satisfied, and once local markets are created, fair trade can begin in earnest (Espa and Marín Durán, 2018).

Fairtrade is an important solution to the problems of globalization because it moves economic activity away from corporate control of production and distribution and toward empowering small businesses. In addition, fair trade creates genuine value from the development of local goods, which drives popular investment in place and reduces consumer waste (Porter and Kramer, 2019). Fairtrade rules must be developed so that all people have equal access to the benefits of fair trade. Fairtrade goods must be made available to everyone who wants them, no matter how rich or poor; every human being must be provided with a basic income. And fair trade must not offer a means for individuals to exploit others from poorer countries and underpay their employees in developing countries.

Globalization and local economy in Local Economies

Globalization has recently risen to the top of the list of hot concerns among the general public and central bankers. Some critics have gone so far as to assert that traditional economic theories of inflation, which pay little attention to globalization, are invalidated by economies being more open to flows of commodities, services, capital, and businesses from other countries (Elhefnawy, 2020). Due to the uneven development, it fosters, globalization is negative for the world economy. Europeans' colonization of Latin America, Africa, and India is perhaps where the idea of globalization first emerged. The start of colonization in the 15th century (Harding, 2019:48-63). Major world powers like Spain and England profited from the wealth of resources available in these new regions. When England supplanted India as the dominant power in 1948, violence, famine, and corruption swept the nation. England kept taxing India heavily and exporting its resources (Sur, 2021).

The global economy has suffered as a result of globalization. Due to capitalism and the availability of cheap labor abroad, countries have been enduring unequal development, exploitation that limits the growth of their economies, and trade wars since colonization (Ayeb and Bush, 2019).

Long-term price stability is what monetary policy aims to achieve and thus promotes maximum sustainable employment and economic growth. The Federal Reserve's short-term goal is to fulfill its twin mandate, stabilizing prices and lowering output volatility and employment near their maximum sustainable levels (Gavin, 2018). Both the behavior of inflation and output as well as the method by which monetary policy influences inflation and output, or the monetary transmission mechanism, are impacted by globalization, which hurts the ability of monetary policymakers to stabilize prices and output.

The main cause of central banks' target price stability is because its main method of stabilizing the economy is through monetary policy (da SILVA, P.E.R.E.R.I.R.A, and L.A.–MOJON, 2019:28-29). Since globalization can impact price stability, it must be considered when determining how much of an impact it will have on monetary policy.

Globalization and inflation

Inflation is the rate at which prices increase. It is important to note that the rate at which prices rise will vary depending on how central banks can control them. For example, suppose a rapid increase in prices occurs due to globalization. In that case, there may not be enough of an impact on monetary policy because it may not be possible for central bankers to affect the inflation rates in the economy (Mancini-Griffoli et al., 2018). If this is the case, central banks may feel they are perfectly able to stabilize the economy.

According to the globalization of inflation hypothesis, more and more external influences impact inflation dynamics. The Phillips curve is one example of a standard inflation model that economists have begun to reevaluate in recent years (Hazell et al., 2022). They have also begun to look more closely at global factors, such as globalization, as a potential explanation for the decreased sensitivity of inflation to domestic determinants. Therefore, traditional inflation models should consider the role of global factors beyond their impact via import prices and domestic indicators of slack.

The observed co-movement of inflation rates among advanced economies (A.E.s) amid the expanding internationalization of products, services, and financial markets sparked interest in the global causes of inflation (Ray and Pal, 2022:189-210). Since 2014, the average headline inflation rate in A.E.s has dropped from approximately 10% in the 1970s to under 2%. But since the early 1990s, globalization has advanced rapidly (Chart 1), considerably impacting how the world economy is structured (Ha, Kose, and Ohnsorge, 2021).

While the impact of external factors on inflation outcomes has received considerable attention, it is also possible to make the case that as the world's economies become more interconnected, shocks in one economy can spread to others, affecting domestic macroeconomic outcomes. In this regard, scholars have examined the idea that globalization may profoundly impact inflation more than merely producing short-term changes in the inflation rate (Zhang et al., 2022). More particular, globalization could affect the more persistent component of inflation across A.E.s by altering the structure of the global economy and hence the process of inflation generation (Dunne, 2014).

There is conflicting empirical data regarding how global slack affects how inflation reacts to domestic cyclical conditions. Early research on the deflationary impacts of globalization was primarily concerned with indicators of global slack. According to Auer, Borio and Filardo (2017), adding global slack to classic benchmark inflation rate equations significantly increases their explanatory power. It can explain cyclical inflation changes among A.E.s (Chen and Siklos, 2020). Global slack is defined as a weighted average of international output gaps. There is a minimal indication that global slack influences domestic inflation, according to Lodge and Mikolajun, who add measures of both global slack and global inflation to a Phillips curve for a panel of A.E.s.

It has been determined that while global inflation played a larger influence throughout the 1970s and 1980s (also known as the Great Inflation period), it played less during times when inflation rates were steadier. According to Bianchi and Civelli (2015), global slack impacts inflation dynamics and is positively correlated with globalization, as measured by trade and financial openness (Bianchi and Civelli, 2015:406-433). However, the authors conclude that "... for the consequences of globalization to be economically relevant, considerable major changes in the degree of openness are required."(Rodríguez-Pose, 2020:371-386)

According to Gillitzer and Simon (2018), analysis, more price flexibility has decreased central banks' capacity to use inflation surprises to increase output. In other words, the Phillips curve will get steeper, making the short-term tradeoff between inflation and unemployment more obvious. As a result, central banks will be less motivated to conduct an excessively expansionary monetary policy that raises inflation, as in the Barro-Gordon (1983) model, to take advantage of the short-run tradeoff between inflation and unemployment (Latsos, 2018:177-215).

Best (2016)claimed that although its overall impact is a priori unclear, globalization may not only affect inflation levels but also alter how enterprises set their prices and, in turn, alter how inflation reacts to domestic conditions. The ability of businesses to pass domestic expenses on to consumers to maintain their competitiveness or market share may be constrained by growing exposure to global competition. However, increased trade integration and openness may adversely affect market concentration and favor bigger, more productive firms that are generally more protective of markups (Lourenco et al., 2021). Although avoiding making causal claims, the data in this box lend support to the idea that a company's ability to pass costs on to customers may be constrained overall by increased exposure to international competition.

Figure 2

Sources: ECB staff calculations, KOF Swiss Economic Institute, and national sources.

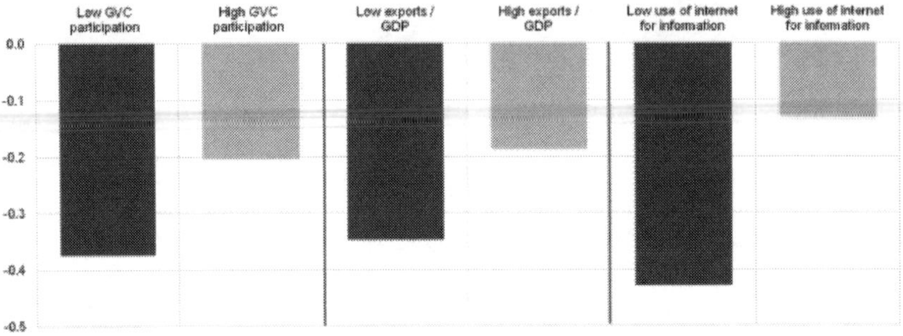

Figure 3: Global factors affecting the slope of price Phillips curves in CEE EU countries.

For the panel of CEE EU members, a higher reliance on export markets and greater VGC involvement are linked to a lesser correlation between inflation and the domestic business cycle (figure, left-hand and middle panels). Compared to observations with comparatively higher VGC involvement and trade openness, the computed coefficients are much lower (Chart A, yellow bars). However, because the cross-country variation (which generates the estimated coefficients shown in Chart A) is smaller than the country-specific time-variation in VGC participation, the contribution of VGC participation in reducing the correlation between activity and prices for individual countries is feasibly minimal.

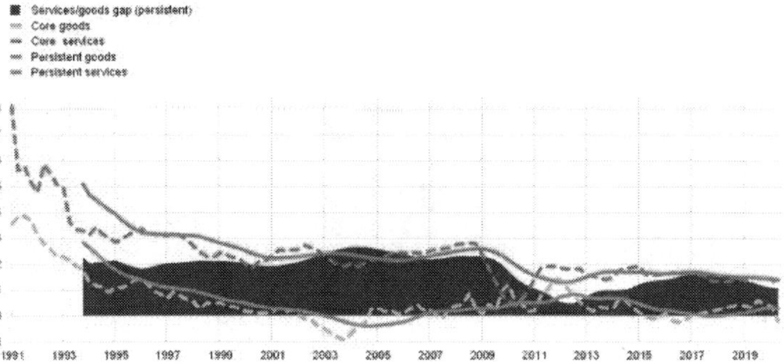

Figure 4

Sources: national sources and ECB staff calculations.

Notes: persistent inflation rates are computed based on 12-quarter moving averages of core goods and services, calculated as the weighted average (GDP purchasing power parity (PPP) weights) of six advanced economies (Australia, Canada, the euro area, Japan, the United Kingdom, and the United States) (Lodge et al., 2021). The latest observation is for Q2 2020.

Because it increases market competition, globalization has the potential to boost product development. If monetary policy does not become more expansionary, higher productivity growth may result in lower pricing, lowering prices directly and cutting inflation (Guerrieri et al., 2021). Furthermore, because output growth will continue to be rapid when inflation is falling, such growth makes it simpler for the monetary authorities to permit inflation to decline.

If China were genuinely exporting deflation, the impact would mostly be seen in how import prices behave. According to research conducted at the Federal Reserve Board by Kamin, Marazzi, and Schindler (2006), purchases of Chinese goods have decreased U.S. import price inflation by about one percentage point annually over the past ten years (Kamin, 2011). This decline has caused a short-term decrease in consumer price inflation of about 0.1 percentage points and a larger effect over the longer term. Pain, Koske, and Sollie's (2006) work at the Organization for Economic Co-operation and Development (OECD) yield a comparable estimate of the impact of trade in manufactured goods with developing nations on U.S. inflation: -0.2 to -0.3 percentage point.

The increased demand for primary commodities from growing Asia, particularly China and India, is also increasing the price of these products globally. Between 2004 and 2006, the region was responsible for more than 70% increase in demand for copper and zinc and around 40% of the increase in world oil consumption (Henckens, 2021). The rise of the Chinese and Indian economies on the world stage has sparked a boom in global commodities.

This has significantly counterbalanced the deflationary impacts of their low-cost goods and services.

The staff's best estimation is that China and India's entry onto the international trading scene has slightly impacted inflation before the recent commodity price boom. Similar findings are drawn from OECD research (Pain, Koske, and Sollie, 2006), which calculates an overall net effect of 0 to - 1/4 percentage point on the economies of the U.S., the euro region, and the OECD.

Cheaper imports from nations like China lower relative prices for imported items. Still, Laurence Ball (2006) points out that they ultimately have no impact on inflation, which is the change in overall prices. Ball notes that for every decrease in the relative price of one commodity or service in a price index such as the consumer price index (CPI), there is by definition a rise in the relative price of a different good or service, following Milton Friedman's line of reasoning (Friedman, 1974).

Any pattern of relative price fluctuations can be accommodated by a specific degree of inflation. The balance between public demand and supply in the economy, ultimately determined by monetary policy rather than relative prices for one category of goods and services, drives the overall inflation rate (Faria-e-Castro, 2021). The ball believes that low-cost imports from China and other low-wage nations shouldn't impact inflation.

Globalization and Manufacturing of local goods

Lund et al. (2019) explained that due to comparative or absolute advantages enjoyed by other nations in particular industries, domestic industries in some nations may be in peril. The overuse and abuse of natural resources to satisfy new, greater demands in creating goods is another potential risk and negative outcome. By decreasing the viability of ecosystems and their essential functions, globalization may significantly negatively influence local commons (Ahmed et al., 2021).

These resources are highly vulnerable to exploitation without strong local institutions, especially when used to supply international markets. Local communities, governments, and sustainable economies can act as a buffer against the harmful consequences of globalization. Local communities are capable of navigating worldwide markets, creating jobs, and maintaining and even enhancing regional biodiversity (Bianchi and de Man, 2021).

In general, popular movements against globalization and globalization have gained prominence in recent years, especially since the onset of the 2008 recession. In governments of almost all countries, political parties have some form of anti-globalization policies. Social movements are becoming increasingly prominent at the grassroots level, with anti-globalization becoming part of the political landscape in European countries such as Spain and Greece (Daphi, 2019:142-154).

A study Garrett by (2014) analyzed that the way that domestic jobs in America are being impacted by foreign manufacturing is another facet of contemporary globalization that has a detrimental effect on the economy. Manufacturing goods in nations like China rather than exporting them to the United States is more affordable due to the availability of inexpensive labor and supplies overseas. Millions of jobs in the United States have been lost due to this change in manufacturing (Charles et al., 2019:307-372). The scale of job losses in America more than 6 million jobs lost as a result of manufacturing shifting to China.

The administration of President Trump is trying to impose protective tariffs on goods imported into the United States from China to counteract this economic shift. They resulted in a trade conflict between China and the United States (Kwan, 2020). Because of capitalism and globalization, American suppliers are now searching abroad for less expensive production. Due to this, America lost millions of jobs, and a trade war with China resulted. Because it pits nations against one another to protect their economies, globalization is harmful to the world economy.

Income Disparity and Globalization

Income inequality, in economic terms, is the wide divergence in income distribution among people, groups, communities, social classes, or nations (Manduca, 2019). Given that it is how we distinguish the top, middle, and working classes, it plays a significant role in comprehending socioeconomic positions.

Competition has risen as a result of globalization. Thousands of people in less developed nations are willing and ready to work for less money than employees in rich nations get paid in exchange for their services. People from the poor world have come to wealthy countries to pursue opportunities in the manufacturing sector, leading to numerous job losses in developed nations (McMillan et al., 2014). Competing with the displaced workers lowers the wages of the remaining employees.

The United States has experienced significant income inequality since the 1940s. However, it reached its peak or grew out of control at the beginning of the twenty-first century. In particular, the income of the majority of impoverished households was almost five times lower at the beginning of the 21st century than that of practically all rich people. Compared to what was documented in the 1980s, this was approximately three times higher (Carlson, Wimer, and Haskins, 2022). Additionally, it is believed that in the 1980s, the United States had a 70% increase in revenue that went directly into the pockets of the wealthy, who at the time made up just 1% of the population (Flaherty and Rogowski, 2021). Over the last two decades, this inequality has gotten worse. For instance, only one percent of Americans were wealthy in the middle of the 1990s. Interestingly, these households held more than 40% of capital market stocks, more than 40% of private and public bonds, and more than 40% of all real estate assets (Yavorsky et al., 2019).

Three steps are taken in the analysis of income inequality within wealthy nations. The post-war boom, which spans from the late 1940s to the early 1970s, is the first phase (Kelly, 2018). On the other perspective, the stagnation phase spans from the early 1970s to the early 1980s.

The new age spans the early 1980s through the middle of the 2000s. In the years following World War II and until the 1960s, many wealthy nations experienced rapid income growth; for instance, in the U.S., earnings for those employed in manufacturing increased by roughly 80%. During the same period, the wealthiest Americans had an increase in income of about 40% (Smith, Zidar, and Zwick, 2021).

The middle class and the wealthy lost income during the era of stagnation that ended in the early 1980s. Because of this, the wealthy's income decreased by around 4%, while wages for workers in the industrial sector fell by roughly 3% (Brandolini et al., 2018). While earnings in categories like the middle class stagnated throughout the new era that preceded the early 2000s, they rose in the richest category. Particularly, income of the wealthy group in the United States increased by about 200 percent between the early 1980s and the mid-2000s. Income inequality in wealthy nations increased in the 1980s, 1990s, and early 2000s but declined slightly after 2007 (Therborn, 2020).

Globalization played a role in the development of this trend by adopting economic reform in these nations during the past 40 years or so. This feature made these countries more accessible to international markets. As a result, trade liberalization was widely embraced in most of these nations, especially in the 1980s and 1990s. It played a significant role in their internationalization (Saavedra-Rivano, 2021). Globalization during this time resulted in fewer trade restrictions. The connection between these changes in income disparity between the wealthiest and the middle class has therefore been examined.

But by the late 1990s, globalization had introduced additional features beyond trade liberalization and trade openness. The economic environment during this time underwent a significant change due to several factors. These factors include increased capital inflows, increased foreign direct investment, exposure to exchange rate fluctuations or changes that negatively affect exports, and immigration-related pressure on local resources, to name a few(Antràs, 2020). These characteristics largely determine how these nations fit into or integrate into the global market.

But by the late 1990s, trade liberalization and openness weren't the only aspects of globalization that had been adopted. Numerous factors, such as higher capital cash flow, risen direct investment from abroad, exposure to exchange rate perturbations or changes that negatively influence exports, and pressure from immigration on local resources, to name a few, led to a significant change in the economic environment during this time(Volz et al., 2020). These qualities significantly determine how these countries fit into or integrate into the global market. One possible source and driving factor for economic inequality over time and between nations is globalization. The wealth gap and inequality between a society's highly educated and less educated citizens may be exacerbated by globalization. As a result of ongoing pressure from globalization, earnings for unskilled workers could be dropping.

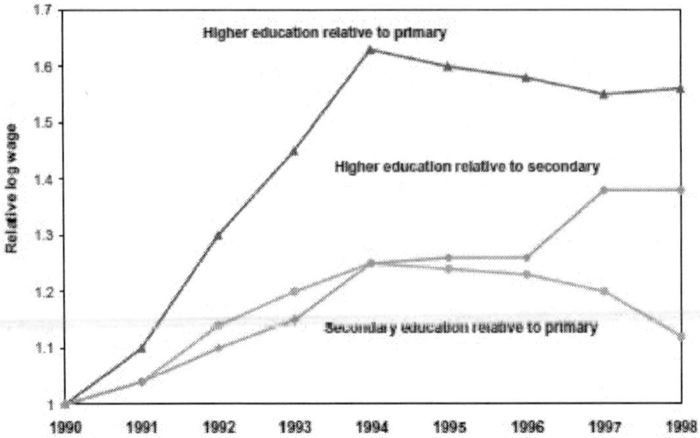

Figure 1 Relative returns to different levels of education in Latin America Source: Behrman, Birdsall and Szekely (2003). 'Economic Policy and Wage Differentials in Latin America.'

Figure 5: Relative returns to different level of education in Latin America

The figure above depicts the average relative rate of return on education for 18 Latin American nations, with higher education returns increasing far more quickly than lower education returns. Global trade markets, cash flows, and technology, particularly the internet, are becoming more linked, which is driving up demand for talents faster than supply globally. This makes national inequality worse; China and India are two good examples. By promoting emigration of highly trained residents, who naturally are most inclined to leave the poorest countries where they are least able to use their abilities effectively, it can further worsen inequality across nations.

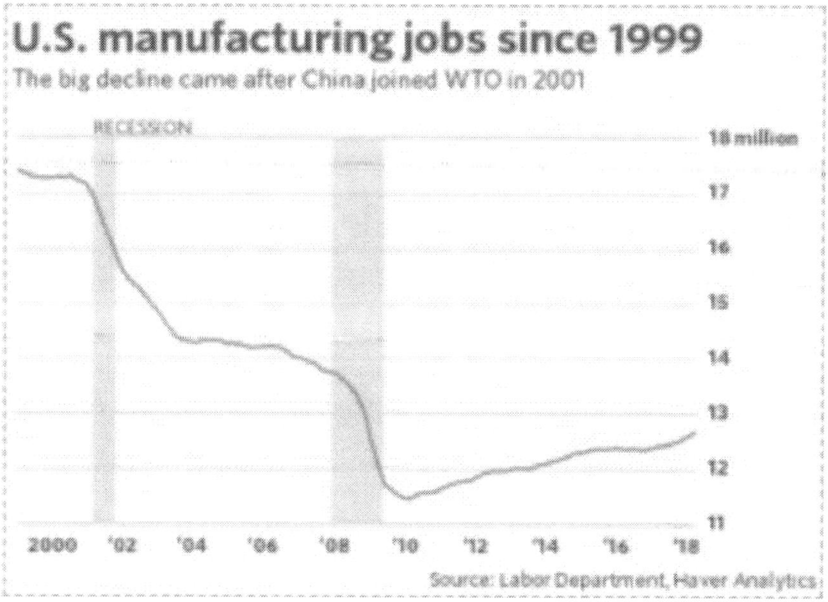

Figure 6: Unemployment in U.S manufacturing jobs since 1999

Globalization and Over dependency

A poor route dependency emerges from globalization's exploitation of developing nations for the advantage of rich nations. According to Martins, 2019, The Development of the Underdeveloped of Latin America is a direct effect of capitalist progress. Only the core nations in Latin America gained as capitalism extended throughout the region, so trading links with their colonists was advantageous for nations like Brazil throughout colonization (Koddenbrock et al., 2020). Developing nations are a source of inexpensive labour and raw materials for core nations. For instance, the coffee trade significantly boosted Brazil's economy during colonialism.

Brazil, however, had a severe economic downturn soon after its modest economic success. This is so because while Brazil was still a colony, its trade with other European nations was steady, but when Brazil became independent, its fledgling economy could not survive (Russell-Wood, 2020). Brazil's route reliance, as a result, has stopped the country's economy from expanding. Brazil was used as a resource to the advantage of European nations. When these nations moved their trade elsewhere, it had a detrimental and long-lasting effect on Brazil's economy (Morgan, Pfaff, and Wolfersberger, 2022). Because it places developing nations on a poor economic trajectory from which they cannot readily reverse, globalization is negative for the world economy and prevents undeveloped nations from progressing.

With a rapid geographic and temporal spread in extraction rates, globalization may lead to an increase in resource exploitation in exporting nations (Martins, 2019). For instance, growing globalization led to the spread of sea urchin exploitation in numerous nations. The quick exploitation of certain energy sources, the use of virtual water, an increase in pollution, the extinction of species, the depletion of fish stocks, and biological invasions are all effects of globalization (Cooke et al., 2021). The potential loss from a double exposure to climatic change and economic globalization is a severe threat, and forest loss and recovery are also at risk.

Growth, Unemployment, and Inequality

There is a wealth of research on the growth effects of globalization and the impact on unemployment and inequality. There is little evidence to suggest that globalization has produced a rise in unemployment comparable to that observed in the 1970s (Stevenson, 2020). Nevertheless, a significant number of studies indicate that globalization increases inequality across nations depending upon factors like income, education level, and country of residence. Nevertheless, most economic studies support the view that globalization raises income growth for workers and consumers, who enjoy lower costs and better-quality products (Erixon, 2018). Furthermore, most research suggests that income gains from trade more than offset its distributional effects.

Less power of local industries

Globalization is said to create room for free access to the world market. This only applies to developed countries since they enact protective measures to maintain their status as developed countries (Hopper, Lassou, and Soobaroyen, 2017). Such protectionism is resisted by developing countries as political resistance to globalization and influence from rich, mainly developed nations. The political resistance of developing countries is not always likely to lead to particular improvements in the efficiency and effectiveness of labor relations. Still, it does lead to increased demand for education, which can be directed toward improving skills and productivity at the local level.

Expansion of communication services, the advantages of globalization in emerging nations, such as Somalia, has not yet been fully realized. The market was overly open, creating a place where products from the industrialized world could be dumped. The situation of the local industry, whose production heavily depends on imported raw materials in the context of unpredictable currency rates, deteriorated due to the government's inability to prevent imported goods from competing with domestically produced comparable items (Helmboldt, West, and Hardy, 2021). The manufacturing sector has been severely damaged, leaving it with no choice except to restructure further, close down, or scale back operations. Economic protectionism is the toughest challenge to globalization being experienced today. The developed world has imposed strict restrictions on capital inflows and outflows, which are, in effect, discouraging investment in developing countries. Seven major trade barriers inhibit globalization of this sort: customs barriers, duties and tariffs, government subsidies, local content rules, local production requirements, and investment restrictions (Labonté, 2019). These measures only serve to limit access to markets for developing nations.

The most important criticism of globalization is its failure to live up to the promise of prosperity for all. According to Joseph Stiglitz, the benefits of globalization are erratic and unevenly spread across countries (Stiglitz 2016). For instance, Mexico's participation in NAFTA has substantially increased exports but only benefited a select few in employment and wages. Globalization has led to the export of low-skilled jobs to lower-wage countries. It has led to an increase in inequality between rich and developing nations while also increasing inequality between rich and poor people within these nations. The gap between rich and poor people has increased since the 1970s, and this trend intensifies as globalization spreads. The International Labor Organization reports that global inequalities have increased by ten times since the 1970s (Alvaredo, 2018).

The critics of globalization are numerous, but few are adamantly opposed to the practice of free trade. Some of these critics include the supporters of protectionism, who argue that developing nations can do far better than participate in free trade. Some critics argue that globalization is a temporary phenomenon, much like the Industrial Revolution, and will eventually be superseded by a new order driven by greater technological change (Alam et al., 2020). One argument advanced by the supporters of protectionism is that countries should be allowed to keep control over their production and export markets. Another argument is that there is a lack of political will to advance democracy and human rights in the developing world, but this does not discourage countries from trading with these nations (Fukuyama, 2018). As a result, there is little reason for the developed world to maintain free trade agreements with developing countries that undemocratic governments often run.

It is evident from various arguments presented by critics of globalization that its failure to improve the lives of people around the world is largely due to ineffective governance. Policymakers of developing nations have consistently suffered from low levels of education and unemployment, making them easy targets for exploitation by unscrupulous international companies (Mogaji and Nguyen, 2021). Although globalization has helped spread knowledge and reduce the cost of communication, the poor have felt very few of these benefits.

The positive economic benefits that are expected from globalization are likely to fade in a few years if the world ignores all the negative effects that it produces. The benefits from globalization have not been distributed equally, which has inevitably led to political resistance in developing countries.

Globalization effects In Africa

Usman et al. (2020) explained that globalization will continue to strengthen the interconnection between many nations and areas. Additionally, it has the potential to strengthen ties between developed nations and the rest of the globe. Additionally, the developed nations might assist in further opening their markets to the goods and services in which the developing world has a comparative advantage to foster this cooperation in a mutually advantageous way. Twerefou, Danso-Mensah and Bokpin, (2017) added that sufficient money under favorable conditions will need to be provided to continue supporting the reform initiatives of the African nations.

It is significant to highlight that the Fund has permanently established the ESAF, our concessional loan instrument, to continue supporting the reform initiatives of the poorest nations, particularly in Africa. Additionally, the World Bank and the Fund have only started putting the framework for action to address the external debt issues of severely indebted low-income countries (HIPC), particularly their significant multilateral debt, into practice. Uganda, Burkino Faso, and Côte d'Ivoire are three of the first nations to be taken into account for the Initiative (Salahuddin, Vink and Gow, 2019).

According Kieh (2016) designing public policies to optimize the distinct benefits of globalization and reduce the downside risks of destabilization and marginalization is a dilemma facing the developing world and African nations. None of these ideas are novel, and most African nations have practiced them for some time. Particularly in sub-Saharan Africa, sustained growth has advanced significantly:

The performance of overall growth has continued to improve. From less than 1% in 1992 to over 5 1/2% in 1996, average real growth has grown, and this encouraging trend is anticipated to continue;

Little progress has been made in bringing inflation down; several nations already have single-digit inflation rates, and for the area as a whole, the average inflation rate is predicted to drop from its peak of 60% in 1994 to 17% in 1997 countries' internal and external imbalances have also decreased. The entire fiscal deficit has decreased from about 12 percent of GDP to 6 percent during the same time, while the foreign currency account deficit has decreased from an average of 15 1/2 percent of GDP in 1992 to roughly 9 percent predicted for this year (Salahuddin et al., 2019).

The openness of African nations' economies to international trade has also advanced significantly (Asongu, 2014). The fact that 31 Sub-Saharan African nations, practically all of them since 1993, have ratified the Fund's Articles of Agreement's duties under Article VIII is a solid indication of this. Most nations have advanced in the liberalization of trade and exchange, doing away with numerous exchange rates, nontariff obstacles and reducing the level of tariff protection.

According to a recent qualitative study by the Fund's African Department, the number of Sub-Saharan African nations with "restrictive" exchange policies fell from 26 in 1990 to only 2 in 1995, while the number of nations with "substantially liberal" trade policies increased from 26 to 38 over the same period (Rafindadi and Usman, 2019). Additionally, most African nations have been lowering the import tariff rates and reducing gasoline prices, but only to a negligible degree.

While it is true that these accomplishments are encouraging, they are far from sufficient. Sub-Saharan Africa's economic performance has generally weakened over the last nine months (Razzu and Wambile, 2022). In 1997, the average annual growth rate of the Sub-Saharan African region was expected to return to its recent track of more than 5% per annum; however, growth in 1997 will be far lower than in 1996, according to Fund staff estimates. The slowdown in Sub-Saharan Africa's economic performance is intensified by the tensions resulting from the global crisis.

Difficulties with external debt and liquidity have aggravated the situation for African nations. Three main external trends are negatively affecting Sub-Saharan Africa's external financing position:

- The deteriorating global and regional economic conditions; the poor performance of the region's export-oriented economies; and • the strong slowdown in world merchandise trade.
- The debt crisis in Nigeria, a major oil exporter, is particularly concerning for Sub-Saharan Africa. This country's external debt and obligations have reached an estimated $80 billion (£43.1 billion).
- The authorities are currently negotiating with multilateral creditors and Paris Club creditors to restructure Nigeria's debt. In recent years, bilateral creditors have provided an additional $6.5 billion (£3.5 billion) to support the country's balance of payments position. The Fund is working closely with the international community to help African nations resolve their difficulties with external debt

and liquidity intensified by the recent global crisis (Lund et al., 2019).

It is becoming more prevalent for African economies to be restructured. Government involvement in economic activities is decreasing across the continent. Agricultural marketing has undergone significant liberalization, and administrative price limitations are being abolished. In most nations, restructuring and privatizing state-owned businesses has been in progress for some time, but it has progressed at varying rates and to varying degrees of success (Passas, 2017). Finally, fiscal reform is progressing; African nations are seriously trying to streamline their tax structures, cut back on exemptions, and improve administrative effectiveness. They are also reallocating funds away from wasteful spending and toward better public investment in and spending on essential social services, most notably health and elementary education.

Globalization's impact in the EU

Globalization has had a great impact on the employment of skilled workers in Europe. This is mainly due to the fact that skilled workers are in very high demand worldwide (Schmidt, 2020). Their wages have increased globally, thereby making their jobs more secure. In addition, globalization has led to greater competition among labor and employers within Europe and internationally. The qualifications and skills of such workers are important, especially their knowledge of the European Union. This is why organizations are requiring its employees to acquire new skills through training programs made available by those employers who hire them on a permanent basis (Berend, 2016)

Although it can sometimes lead to employment losses, globalization opens up new work chances. The EU prioritizes managing globalization to maximize its benefits and working to build a more social Europe that aids jobless people in finding new employment. However, it is important to ask whether the EU should allow free movement of workers between EU members and be able to offer their services anywhere within the EU (Asteriou Dimelis and Moudatsou, 2014)

An increasing number of employment are being directly or indirectly supported by EU exports outside the union. From 21.7 million employees in 2000 to 36 million jobs in 2017, it rose. An average of 13,000 EU jobs is supported for every billion in EU exports. Jobs aren't just available in exporting businesses. They encompass businesses that provide goods and services to them as well (Surugiu and Surugiu, 2015). For instance, 6.8 million employments in Germany are supported by exports to nations outside the EU. Thanks to the EU single market, exports from other EU nations to non-EU countries support an additional 1.1 million employment in Germany. In Germany, exports to the EU support 18% of all jobs.

Because of the increasing rivalry between businesses brought on by globalization, there may be closures, outsourcing, and job losses. The manufacturing, textile, apparel, footwear, and leather industries, as well as the basic metals and fabricated metal products industries, are the most susceptible EU sectors. Manufacturing is the industry most vulnerable to offshore due to competition from nations with cheap wages (Rodrik, 2018).

The Covid-19 outbreak has highlighted the necessity of relocating crucial industries and goods, such as pharmaceuticals, to Europe (Aslan and Altinoz, 2021). The trend of outsourcing has changed, and eastern European nations now experience more of it than do western EU members. North Africa and Asia are the destinations. Although international trade liberalization has generally beneficial consequences, certain industries have been heavily damaged, and the length of the adjustment time required for people to migrate in other industries might reduce the early advantages (Ramsfield et al., 2016)

How to reduce Globalization

I. Microeconomics Policies

Policymakers have three realistic alternatives to try to lessen these conflicts and difficulties. Microeconomic policies come first and are the most crucial. They involve using trade, business, and finance policies to improve the international competitive position of firms, industries, and nations. Macroeconomic policies are second and are intended to shape the international economy; fostering open markets while keeping it fair (Gillitzer and Simon, 2018).

Structural policies come third and are geared toward strengthening the "soft infrastructure" that under girds Globalization (Carroll, Gonzalez-Vicente, and Jarvis, 2019:778-803). Increasingly, this includes developing countries' human capital - their people's skills training and education - to complement investments in hard infrastructures, such as technology centers, ports, and bridges. Another form of structural policy is establishing a basic social safety net to protect workers from disruptions caused by Globalization.

Globalization and macroeconomic policies are used to smooth out domestic fluctuations in output. They are also a way to coordinate economic activity with other countries. Finally, global macroeconomic policies stabilize the world economy as a whole. These policies can be implemented by the International Monetary Fund, which has seen its power and responsibilities increase to foster stability and growth (Gaspar et al., 2019). The IMF is funded by its 185 member countries, which each contribute a proportion of their currency's value based on their gross domestic product (Mehedintu, Soava, and Sterpu, 2019:212). This encourages countries to contribute financially because they become members with greater voting power when they do so. Then the IMF lends the money to countries experiencing serious issues with declining currency values and needing aid. This spurred a wave of post-World War II international cooperation and coordination (Konadu-Agyemang and Takyi, 2018:17-24).

Another group facilitating international economic cooperation is the World Trade Organization, which aims to promote a fair-trading system. It currently has 148 member countries committed to reducing barriers to world trade, functioning as a forum for negotiations, and encouraging multinational enterprises (Chow, 2020:599). It publishes international agreements concerning standards nations should follow when negotiating trade agreements with other countries. The WTO also has a dispute settlement process.

The WTO's ultimate goal is to increase worldwide economic growth and bring prosperity to the poor (Bianchi and de Man, 2021). It wants to make the global economy more productive to create more jobs, reduce poverty, and allow people to live better lives.

Devastating effect of globalization on local economies by loss of local production/blue collar job

According to Dr. Robert Neild, local economies are dependent on the global market. He believes that because of this, industries will always be in competition with other sectors and that, in order to survive, they must find ways to improve their performance against the rest of the world. If this happens, then countries will be able to retain their economic control over the areas within their borders. As it stands now, even though local industries are undoubtedly dependent on the global market, the reverse is certainly not true (Aslan, A. and Altinoz, 2021)

This is because countries are more dependent on their local sectors for employment and tax revenue. Brown (2014) claimed that if a country loses control of its local economy to foreign powers, it will have to shift from a protectionist stance to an open-market policy in order to compete with other trade nations for business. This is exactly what has happened in the United States.

Maley (2019) explained that globalization has changed the structure of jobs, the distribution of economic activities. Globalization has promoted relocation of production and changes in the international division of labor. Due to shifting competitive advantages and patterns of specialization, employment associated with some economic activities may tend to disappear while jobs associated with other, perhaps new activities are created. Via a greater pace of job creation and destruction as well as through the rising prevalence of informal and precarious work, globalization is reducing employment security Monarch, Park and Sivadasan (2014) added that the blue-collar labor markets have been greatly affected by structural changes associated with globalization. In many countries, the wages of skilled workers have increased, but the wages of less skilled workers have decreased. Because such workers are in higher demand, their wages have also increased.

A study by Lawal (2020) explained that the middle-class jobs may also change due to globalization. Since companies are expanding, middle-class positions emerge that include positions of management and top executives at the middle level. Thus, a skilled worker's job has been converted into a middle-class position and it is reflected in the salaries paid to such workers. The salaries of less skilled workers drop as those jobs become more skilled intensive and white collar jobs.

In most countries according to Fowler (2014), it is observed that low wages are associated with globalization. The wages of unskilled workers are much lower than that in advanced economies. The wages of skilled workers also tend to be lower in developing countries, but their incomes generally have increased compared with earlier years. Moreover, the average skill level among higher-skilled workers is high in developed countries while average skill levels are low in developing countries.

Ragheb, El-Shimy and Ragheb (2016) added that by decreasing the viability of ecosystems and their essential functions, globalization may have a significant negative influence on local commons. These resources are highly vulnerable to abuse without strong local institutions, especially when used to supply international markets. Local communities are generally aware of the threats to their economic well-being, such as the overfishing of local seas and rivers, or the careless logging of forests. In some cases, their response has been to curtail the use of local resources, leading to a reduction in income for the people who rely on these resources for employment. This results in what is known as an 'empty forest syndrome', in which "communities are reduced to waiting for outside intervention" (Gilbert et al., 1997). In other cases, local communities may protect and maintain their resources in ways that are consistent with their culture and indigenous practices; however, these can conflict with the purposes of global markets. The multistate ecosystem framework

(MEF), which Randhir (2016) introduced, includes data on ecological elements, socioeconomic activities, and their interconnections.

Xiaoman et al., 2021 analyzed the effects of globalization on the local economy. Despite globalization increasing the lives of people it has its negative effects too. Globalization often lowers the cost of production. This implies that businesses may charge customers less for their products. One important factor that raises the level of life is the average cost of commodities. Additionally, consumers have access to a greater range of items.

The authors gave an example of Bangladesh's garment industry. It produces clothing that is subsequently exported all over the world. Despite having up to four million employees, the typical worker makes less money in a month than an employee in the United States does in a day. Bangladesh's economy has also suffered because it has not been able to keep up with international competition. Amin (2017) explained that globalization often increases the chances of a local economy suffering from poor policies, such as environmental pollution, business practices that are unfair to workers, or poor education and training standards. This can lead to higher rates of crime and violence.

Rembet et al., 2014 analyzed the impact of globalization on local industries. The study used Mogandishu as the case study.

Globalization is a subject that many writers have discussed, but in the context of Somalia it is obscured by other similar issues, therefore this research looked at how the industrial sector in Mogadishu handled it. A majority of respondents strongly agreed that they were dependent on imported raw materials from other countries. The study also discovered that electricity was a significant barrier that was too expensive for these manufacturers, and that raw materials were the most difficult issues facing the manufacturing sector. The survey, however, also showed that these manufacturers have some positive strength when it comes to marketing and sales, since most of them thought that there was a market for what they produced and that consumers preferred their products over imports.

Thompson & Wadley, (2018) explained that More is lost than just the hundreds (or thousands) of jobs that leave the country when a local plant shutters as a result of a company's decision to outsource to a supplier across the border. Reduced expenditure on local products and services multiplies the effects, which affects employees and employers throughout the local economy. Tax revenues for the local government decrease as well, leaving less money for public services like education. Family dissolution, opiate addiction, and other societal evils frequently accompany anomie. In manufacturing, the multiplier effect of globalization on the local economy is, by far, its most significant economic impact. (Thompson and Wadley, 2018).

Ocloo, Akaba and Worwui-Brown (2014) claimed that the business world has reached a turning point in history due to globalization, increased competitive pressure, and rapid technological advancements. As a result, the Small and Medium Enterprise (SMEs) sector in Africa and Ghana has been hardest hit and is currently facing new challenges as they work to expand their operations globally and become competitive. The goal of this study was to determine how many the difficulties hinder Ghana's small and medium-sized firms' ability to compete globally. The study found that the degree of competition and advancing technology had a significant impact on globalization and the competitiveness of SMEs. The report advised SMEs to implement the appropriate strategies in order to adapt to the changing conditions in the global market space.

A study by Kramsch (2014) showed that Globalization have brought competition between local products and foreign. This has reduced the value of the locally produced gods this is because they are competing with foreign products which have increased the value of the imports. This has also led to poor domestic businesses because they have to compete with foreign imports in this local economy confirmed by Asshidin, Abidin and Borhan

(2016). The government suffers from the effects of globalization and their policy responses are often ineffective. There is also a high level of unemployment which reduces the demand for locally produced services and the value of the local currency.

Ebenstein, et al., 2014 claimed that globalization has led to the loss of jobs that are both in manufacturing and services. This has resulted in a reduction in supply of labor which increases wages, thus affecting employment. Employers have been forced to downsize their work forces due to the increased availability of labor in industrialized countries and Third World countries. However, it has also led to much greater competition in many industries. This has reduced the profits that many businesses can make and has negatively affected the well-being of employees and the economic stability of their local communities.

Bretos & Marcuello (2017) evaluated the effects of globalization on local markets along with the social, economic, and political implications. This paper is a contribution to an increasingly broad body of research that has focused on the impacts of globalization in different parts of the world. The main focus is on how globalization impacts local markets by examining two main areas; that is, how it affects their survival and role as a source of employment.

Globalization can be a major threat to small businesses which may lead to their ultimate demise. The problem arises when local companies are unable to compete with the threat posed by foreign competitors. This is especially true for industries in which there are significant economies of scale and/or firms face regulatory disadvantages due to transportation costs, government services, and property rights protection.

The paper argues that globalization leads not only to the collapse and extinction of some local corporations but also affects employment. Small-sized businesses can either survive by adopting and competing with foreign companies or be replaced by them. Thus, globalization not only affects local economies but also the local labor market, and generally this means that a few people will lose their jobs due to the loss of business to foreign competition.

On blue collar jobs, the process of globalization can lead to loss of jobs in services and manufacturing. This has resulted in a reduction in supply of labor which increases wages, thus affecting employment. The problem is that many employers have been forced to downsize their workforces due to the increased availability of labor in industrialized countries and Third World countries. Globalization not only affects the local economies but also the local labor market. It thus implies that some people lose their jobs as a result of the loss of business to foreign competition. This also leads to a reduction in household income and demand for goods and services, which ultimately affects the local economy.

Due to increasing pressure from multinational corporations and industry associations that are becoming more powerful and imposing their own conditions of purchase regardless of the actual production costs incurred by producers, globalization has made it harder for farmers in developing countries to negotiate better terms.

Globalization has changed the trade agenda dramatically. It has been argued that globalization might pave the way for the development of an open and democratic trading system. However, it has proved to be quite the contrary as it has emerged as a source of instability and conflict. In this regard, Vormelker (2005) noted that in many developing countries, participation in international markets is mirrored by a significant decline in poverty rates and a steady growth of middle-class incomes.

Bardhan et al., 2004 analyzed the role of high tech-firms in globalization. The study addressed global production and marketing and the resultant cognition challenges faced by these companies. In one of the chapter the authors looked at the process of global outsourcing and the impact of it has on the job employment inequality and the value it will add to the economy. In the manufacturing sector in the United States, the salary disparity between blue-collar (production) and white-collar (non-production) workers increased from around $7,500 in 1980 to about $24,000 in 2000.In California, where the pay disparity expanded from around $10,000 to over $30,000 over the same time, a similar and more severe dynamic has been in motion. Nearly three million manufacturing jobs have been lost in the US as a whole over this time, with blue-collar employees accounting for the majority of those losses. Even though this trend of increasing pay disparity has been thoroughly documented, economists disagree on what the causes are.

Some believe that the expanding forces of globalization—international commerce and investment overseas, with the former displacing manufacturing jobs and the latter merely exporting them—are responsible for between one-sixth and one-third of the rising disparity. Others feel the impact of globalization is insignificant and attribute the phenomena of rising inequality to technology advancements or even exogenous changes in consumer tastes and product needs. There is no denying, however, that a number of economic and political factors, including the shifting nature of manufacturing in the United States, the emergence of fierce manufacturing competition abroad, the dominance of services in national output, and others, have all contributed to this phenomenon. Over the past few decades, foreign outsourcing has accelerated, especially in the heavily traded high-tech industries.

A study by Tan (2014) explained that a produced high-tech product's broad value chain, or the number of intermediary goods, services, and production procedures that go into the finished product, is in reality one of its distinguishing characteristics. The fragmented character of manufacturing has substantially risen because to advancements in standards, communications, and transportation. The high-tech value chain is now a multilateral, international manufacturing mosaic.

A study done by Ake (2019) on precarious work stated thatMworkers have been adversely affected by globalization. This has happened due to a variety of factors both in the core and the periphery. The most prominent of these is that globalization has been characterized by increased capital mobility leading to an increase in international unemployment. This can be seen with the process of liberalization whereby policy reforms aim at liberalization and deregulation thus increasing the incentives for firms to move production and jobs abroad. The rise in insecure employment and job polarization are two trends cited by many analysts as examples of how shifting workplace relations are being influenced by economic globalization. Due to job polarization as stated by Rodrick (2018), middle-class occupations, particularly tradable and routine tasks that are readily offshored to lower-wage nations, are losing out in the globalized economy, driving the people who lose out toward insecure employment.

Research from the US done by Kamin (2011) demonstrated that when other car factories shift portion of their international ventures, workers in the auto sector are compelled to accept lower earnings and unstable employment. 31 Affiliate operations set up in Europe, where salaries and working conditions are more or less the same or even higher lessen the severity of this danger. However, the majority of company relocations take place in developing nations, which puts pressure on salaries and working conditions to decline. According to Alexander, (2020), this translates to businesses having an advantage when negotiating lower wages with trade unions for the existing workers and using this situation to alter the relationship between employer and employee. Businesses that find it easier to relocate to regions with lower labor costs have this advantage. The likelihood of a company relocating to a region where labor is cheaper than to one with higher labor costs makes it more likely that the latter has to move toward more precarious forms of employment.

Conclusively, the extent of globalization has forced many developing countries to compete with others in terms of financial, foreign exchange, and capital reserves. Thus, they are being forced to liberalize interest rates and deregulate their economies. Increasing price competition inevitably leads companies to focus on maximizing profit and in the process sheds some of their responsibility towards worker welfare while the state assumes less responsibility towards its citizens (Autio, Mudambi and Yoo, 2021). Ultimately, this will lead to increased exploitation of workers by their employers as it is likely that they will turn towards more precarious forms of employment. However, the role of the state is not limited to deregulation and liberalization of their economies but also to protect its citizens.

China contributing to globalization while maintaining strong local economies Merga & Haji (2019) claimed that China has taken on a leading role in global trade, but it's because of their immense domestic market demand. China is the world's largest exporter as well as its second-largest importer. As such, China has outsourced much of its manufacturing and construction to lower-wage countries. The country also imports a large number of resources from abroad and exports what it produces more cheaply than any other nation. In the process, it has become one of the world's largest economic forces. But China's economic strength has largely been at the expense of its low-wage workers (Hopewell, 2015). Monopoly capitalism and a massive export economy have left China's labor markets very unstable and prone to major upheavals. In fact, it is only by being able to take advantage of cheap foreign labor that China is able to compete with other global powers. This is a major problem.

China's economy has been growing rapidly since the 1980s. This period has seen the growth of free-market capitalism and it has also seen China shift its focus from agricultural production to export-oriented manufacturing. The country's exports fell in relation to its imports, but China still remains the world's largest exporter and second-largest importer respectively. This trend could not continue indefinitely, but China's economy continues to grow each year by more than 10% (Hopewell, 2015). The country has also seen GDP growth from just over 8% in early 2007 to nearly 10% at the beginning of 2008. As of the second quarter, China's economy was about 22 trillion yuan. China's economy is still a major concern for many in the world today, but it is still not too much to be ignored.

Lin & Wang (2018) explained that one extremely important measure of China's participation in globalization is its economy. "China became the greatest exporter in the world in 2010" (CIA World Factbook). Without China, numerous nations, including the United States of America, wouldn't import the billions of dollars' worth of goods from China each year. People have been able to migrate to cities and find employment as a result of an inflow of businesses transferring their production to China. The previous several decades have seen an exponential growth in China's economy. China's GDP has increased by around 10% annually during the past three years. Despite this, there have been a lot of negative effects in China as well.

Rabab et al. (2020) explained that the main reason why China has been able to handle the negative effects of Globalization is because China has a closed economy and has a limited number of imports. As a result, the country has been able to increase its GDP by 10% annually by maintaining its domestic market demand, which allows the country to import the resources it needs from other countries. The country's economy is basically all about exports, so even with all of the negative effects, China can still maintain strong growth in their economy; for example, if oil prices go up or if factory output increases there will be more imports received from other countries (Rababah et al., 2020).

China technological advancements is another reason China is able to use globalization and still keep its economy strong; for example, China has been importing technology toys from other countries such as robots and computer components, which have allowed factories to have more efficiency and productivity (Gilli, & Gilli, 2018). Since China has been importing a lot of technology from other countries, there have also been a lot of new jobs created within the country's labor market. Also, since China has been leading the "race" for new discoveries with many smart technologies imported from other countries, their research and development expenditures are about 70% of the U.S. R&D spending ratio. The country's rapid technological advancements will soon allow them to overtake the United States' global economic power, and can also be used to help lower their production costs, making it more affordable for them to buy resources from other countries (Brooks & Wohlforth, 2015).

A study done by Law (2014) claimed that introduction of reform by China government is the main reason for strong hold of China Globalization. China started implementing significant economic changes in 1979. Farmers were given ownership and price incentives by the central government, which allowed them to sell a part of their harvests on the open market. In order to increase exports, attract foreign investment, and import high-tech goods into China, the government has constructed four special economic zones along the shore. Additional changes, which came gradually afterward, aimed to decentralize the formulation of economic policy in a number of industries, particularly commerce.

According to Liu, Dunford & Gao (2018), provincial and local governments were granted economic power over a variety of businesses, and these governments were typically permitted to operate and compete on free market principles rather than under the direction and control of state planning. Additionally, people were urged to create their own enterprises. Consequently, foreign companies were granted the right to form joint ventures with Chinese firms, and these ventures have since been allowed to trade with each other on a market basis. With each new group of policies for economic reform, China's economy has grown stronger (Brødsgaard, 2014).

Globalization has helped China's economy grow steadily and healthily, and China has also given globalization fresh life according to Xu & Xia (2019). The adoption of cutting-edge technology, management know-how, outside competition, and technical innovation have improved China's total factor productivity and economic growth, particularly following China's WTO membership. GDP increased from USD 189 billion in 1980 to USD 12.2 trillion in 2017, making about 15% of the world's GDP. China has benefited from globalization while also making a sizable contribution to its expansion. China made an average yearly contribution of nearly 30% to the development of the world economy between 2012 and 2016. China has also kept its own markets open to foreign goods and services. As a result, China is the world's largest exporter and second-largest importer respectively.

According to Wang (2015), establishing financial industry policies in China have played a significant role in the country's economy's ability to expand gradually since its reform in 1979.The years after the Great Helmsley Bank of New York, which was one of the first banks to open its doors to Chinese businessmen, have seen more and more foreign banks allow Chinese citizens easier access to their financial services. It aggressively promotes the Belt and Road Initiative and looks at alternative avenues for liberalizing the financial sector. According to Lin (2017), this increased the financial institutions' soundness and competitiveness and prompted the adoption of significant financial sector reforms. The primary goals were to increase competition within the financial industry and bring back the profitability of the sector to a reasonable level in order to close the wealth gap. China has a central bank that is independent from politics, and it also has bankruptcy laws that allow banks to go bankrupt without being bailed out (Lin (2017).

A study done by Zheng et al. (2014) claimed that China government spending on the economy has enabled strong local economies that have been able to remain strong for over 30 years.

The Chinese economy has significantly improved as a result of yuan exchange rate fluctuations and government control over big corporations. Its rules governing foreign companies have also been beneficial.

Tan (2014). Explained that the shift in interest rates and currency instability has been conducive to growth. The strong government has also created an environment where money can be made easily. Money can be made by providing foreign companies with opportunities to create growth within China's vast markets, increasing the productivity of Chinese workers and increasing the amount of revenue that goes towards funding infrastructure projects (Tan, 2014).

Alternative explanations for the strong hold of China's economy are that government foreign aid and subsidies are what allowed their economy to grow so quickly. The government has been doing things like providing a cheap labor force and land so that foreign companies can have access to these things at reasonable prices. A study done by Zeng, (2015) claimed that foreign businesses tend to move their production facilities to China because they get a lot of advantageous resources and subsidies in the country. The government has also been investing heavily in order to allow China's infrastructure to grow, especially in the field of transportation so that people can get their products made and shipped easily. The Chinese government has been funding upgrades in its industries, and it has focused on locating high-tech firms within China so that they can create more jobs and be more effective with their management strategies (Zheng et al., 2015).

Xie, Zhang, and Lai (2014) claimed that China's economy has been able to grow steadily and healthily for the last four decades due to its rapid growth but also its high population. The country has a rapidly growing population, and many people were able to find jobs in the late 20th century. The economy of China has been able to grow steadily because of the large labor force that it provides to foreign companies, allowing more work to be done than ever before. The Chinese government has been protecting the ability of Chinese companies, which contributes heavily to why China is so strong economically.

Chatterji et al. (2015) explained that China has been able to grow steadily in the last thirty years due to a large labor force, flexible labor laws, great markets, and a favorable exchange rate. Because of all of these factors, China is able to save more money than it spends which contributes heavily to why China is so strong economically. The GDP of China has grown steadily over the last thirty years because their economy has been able to produce sufficient amounts of goods and services.

China has emerged as one of the leading lights in global innovation during the past ten years. It invests more than 2.2 percent of GDP on R&D, which is more than the average for the European Union. It also ranks first in the world for local inventions and has made revolutionary strides in important fields like high-speed trains, e-commerce, and digital money. At the cutting edge of global technology are a growing number of Chinese companies. The Chinese government sees innovation as one of the major forces guiding its future development and bringing it closer to more advanced nations. It encourages a relatively free market for its companies. Most of the innovation has focused on information technology.

China has taken some reforms to handle the issue of existing downfalls in its innovation system and ensure that productivity is increased. Wang (2015) explained that the quality of patents has improved, fundamental research has received more funding, and public support for innovation is now better targeted thanks to robust performance incentives and oversight. China might also work more to promote the spread of technology and hasten the modernization of management techniques. And last, China would be wise to maintain the open innovation system that has helped it achieve economic and technical success over the years (Wang, 2015).

China in global market is more than ever before. Its exports expanded from $20 billion in 1991 to $298 billion in 2001, making China the third-largest exporter in the world. In 2002, it became Asia's largest trading partner with its neighbors after surpassing Japan. China has also become a major player in international financial markets and one of the largest investors in foreign countries (Tan, 2014).

The end result is that China has been investing heavily in its infrastructure, tourism and manufacturing sectors. However, the often-cited statistic that China's manufacturing sector is set to become the world's largest by 2010 (although for the moment only accounting for 12%) is highly misleading. This statistic does not reflect a shift from export-led to domestic manufacturers.

There are many people who believe that China's move toward industrialism is bringing about social disruption in Chinese society and will continue to do so as China develops further (Lin & Wang, 2018). China's spectacular economic growth over the past two decades has been predominantly fuelled by export-led mass production industries, in tandem with the economic reforms set in motion by Deng Xiaoping - these were his famous Four Modernizations: agriculture, industry, science and technology and national defense. China's opening up to the world economy has been compared to that of Japan some 20 years previously, which triggered its period of unprecedented overseas expansion (Lin & Wang, 2018).

India

India as a whole has been significantly and almost immediately impacted by globalization. The elimination of import restrictions and export subsidies allowed for unfettered commerce, which greatly increased the appeal of the untapped Indian market to the rest of the world (Roy et al., 2020). These reforms had their greatest impact on the industrial, financial, and agricultural sectors of the country, among other places. One of the nations that had tremendous success following the start and execution of globalization is India. The country is seeing a huge increase in foreign investment in the corporate, retail, and scientific sectors.

Kumar et al., 2022 added that it had a significant influence on social, financial, cultural, and political spheres. Due to advancements in information technology and transportation, there has been a surge in globalization recently. Global trade, doctrines, and culture are all growing as global synergies get better.

India's response to global trade integration has been much more nuanced. Cooke et al., 2014 analyzed the Indian economy. The study claimed that the country is currently experiencing a period of rapid economic growth, referred to as India's "economic miracle" or "economic transformation". Traditional agricultural products, including cotton, paddy and jute, have been largely supplanted by textiles and information technology. The newfound income from industrial exports has also helped fuel economic growth in the 1990s by reducing the need for imports. Hopewell, K., 2015 added that at the same time, major advances in telecommunications and information technology have made India a hub for software development services and outsourcing. Overall, India can be seen as a leader in globalization and is playing an important role in global economic integration.

Willis et al., 2015 claimed that although there has been significant growth due to economic liberalization, the Indian government is reluctant to dismantle regulatory measures that protect agricultural producers. The country's agriculture sector currently employs roughly half of its population, with rice being by far the largest agricultural crop by revenue. The Indian economy's globalization has improved the state of the global economy. Additionally, it gives foreign businesses the chance to gain access to sizable labor and consumer markets, giving rise to an appealing opportunity for strategic investment and growth (Williswt al., 2016)

Liberalization

Malik and Prasad, 2015 defined Liberalization as the process of removing obstacles or limitations imposed by the government. Businesses are free to decide what they want to import or export thanks to trade liberalization. Since there are much less limitations now than there formerly were, the government is considered to be more liberal. The powerful and influential businesses have gained more power because they now have the ability to keep out competitors.

India's participation in international trade has grown exponentially since its liberalization in 1991. The World Trade Organization (WTO) reports that India's annual export growth rate from 1998 to 2001 was nearly 27%, according to Tien, Phu and Chi, (2019) making it the second fastest growing country in the world. Over the past decade, India's average annual export growth has been roughly 17%. Ongoing economic reforms are expected to further accelerate this trend. Bagli and Adhikary (2014) explained that by addressing high trade barriers and reducing its overall tariff rate, India is positioning itself as an attractive destination for foreign direct investment.

Developed Infrastructure

Raichurkar and Ramachandran, 2015 claimed that the country's infrastructural development and industrial progress has also helped improve its competitiveness within the global economy. India has promoted the creation of a wide range of industries, which are now quite competitive with other countries in Asia, Europe and North America. Economic liberalization led to higher productivity growth and higher levels of investment throughout the country. India is a major exporter of software and information technology, in particular to Europe and the United States. The country's information technology industry provides India with large foreign currency reserves as well as large-scale employment opportunities (Raichurkar and Ramachandran, 2015).

Bigger Market

India's semiconductor market expected to reach over $2 billion in 2008 – is among the world's fastest growing markets for this industry according to Siddiqui (2016).Over the next few years, India will spend $4 billion on semiconductor imports. India's pharmaceutical market is also quite large, with an expected growth rate of about 18% annually (Nolan, 2014). The country is also one of the world's largest producers of cotton. In 2004, India became the largest producer of oranges and ranks second in production of bananas.

India has been able to benefit from globalization by using its comparative advantage and capitalizing on what it has to offer. The country is currently a net exporter within many different industries, including petroleum products and software services (Raichurkar and Ramachandran, 2015). The country's reduction in tariffs and increased labor productivity has enabled it to export more and import less.

Lacal-Arántegui, R., 2019. Claimed that the economy's overall growth has been significantly impacted by the economic adjustments that have been implemented. It also signaled the beginning of India's economic integration with the world economy. When foreign currency reserves fell to $1 billion in 1991, the Indian economy was in serious trouble. Numerous industries, including the agricultural, industrial, financial, and health sectors, were impacted by globalization. India's progress in a number of areas didn't start until Man Mohan Singh, the country's then-finance minister, introduced the Liberalization, Privatization, and Globalization (LPG) strategy.Lechner, and Boli, 2020 claimed that The government's commitment to globalization has led to the creation of several new business opportunities for foreign investors, including in the high-tech industry.

Technology

Stearns (2020) explained that one important aspect that has accelerated the trend of globalization is the quickening pace of technological advancement. For instance, there have been several advancements in transportation technology during the last 50 years. Due to this, it is now able to distribute things over great distances considerably more quickly and affordably. There are also improvements being made in the means of communication and in turn this has helped globalization to happen. This has enabled even local economies to benefit from the global economy.

A study done by Korotayev and LePoire, 2020, analyzed that, despite the global implications of technology, local Industries still remain strong. For instance, India is a hub for exporting textiles and iron ore which has enabled the country to remain pro-active in the technological sphere. The idea of employment with better benefits, greater flexibility and increased pay at work has helped globalization expand rapidly. Pradhan 2015 added that the idea of flexi-time pay, telecommuting and job sharing enables people to work from home if they would like or flexibly schedule their working hours. Globalization has made it possible for people to work from home as opposed to commuting and consequently this has helped create a number of jobs that could not have been created before.

India's recent economic growth has been attributed largely to its ability to focus on economic reform and foreign investment. The country has seen large increases in exports due to its liberalized economy and large internal markets for B2B commerce via new media channels. Additionally, India's government is investing heavily in infrastructure development. The country's liberalization has sparked significant foreign investment from countries around the world. It has also attracted a number of global companies to set up shop in India. In particular, information technology and service industries are flourishing, largely due to their large numbers of well-educated English-speaking workers and low labor costs.

Over the long term, India's growing economic prosperity will likely strengthen its global position within the economic system by supporting greater global economic integration.

Since India's economic integration into the world economy in 1991, it has experienced rapid growth. It significantly affects India's economic situation. From 1990 to 1980, its average yearly rate increased from 3.5% to 7.7%. (2002–2012). From 2005 to 2008, that rate reached a peak of 9.5%. The gross domestic product (GDP) per capita has also increased as a result of economic expansion, rising from $1,255 in 1978 to $3,452 in 2005, and eventually to $8,358 in 2022. The International Monetary Fund

(IMF) estimates India will reach a GDP per capita of $3,811 in 2010 and $7,326 in 2025. India's economy is expected to grow at an annual rate of 10.5% until 2010.

The Indian government has made it clear that they favor a particular brand of globalization tailored to the country, one in which the substance, order, and timing of policy actions are modified to minimize any possible negative shocks and maximize the advantages of cross-border integration. The perceived risk-return trade-off has served as the basis for this cautious strategy.

India has had an impressive amount of capital throughout its history, including fertile agricultural land, thriving market towns and long-distance trade routes, fabulously wealthy Nagar Seths and operational small-scale manufacturing enterprises, palaces and other elite extravagances. However, its life and culture were shaped by political leaders and religious figures rather than business moguls. Therefore, for the great majority of Indians, even millionaires and billionaires, capitalism is a comparatively recent cultural force. Indians still have fond memories of Queen Victoria, Akbar the Great, and Ashoka, but there are no capitalists in their cultural pantheon, despite the fact that global corporations like Liptons were present in Indian marketplaces for many years prior to 1947.

Under the British Raj, India was one of the most advanced economies in Asia due to its strong industrial base. The repeal of the British East India Company's trade monopoly in 1833 and the Industrial Revolution were significant contributors. Imports of machine tools, textile machinery, and an extensive railway system from Britain transformed Indian production methods. The availability of cheap labour and capital also contributed. India's export-oriented economy established a pattern of heavy imports (mainly of cotton textiles) and high rates of capital emigration overseas.

The Indian state is a key player in the globalisation process. The Indian state is not only engaged in world trade, but it also takes part actively in global governance. The Indian state is strongly committed to the United Nations (UN), international obligations, and regional and global cooperation. The Indian state has recently strengthened its cooperation with the UN through its membership in various institutions such as the Security Council and various agencies of the UN system, such as UNESCO. It also offers substantial funding for UN-affiliated programmes within the country.

Keohane and Nye, 2020 claimed that "the globalization process is taking place in three key stages: (1) globalization occurs because of global political and economic forces, (2) the state's role changes, and (3) countries increasingly make their own choices about participation in the process." The Indian state has been involved in globalization since its inception. India's reach around the world is wide and deep, far more so than any other major country.

Globalization into Localization

In order to mitigate the effects of Globalization, Localization is suggested as the way to go. Localization is defined as the reversal of globalization and its effect on production and consumption in both developed and developing countries (Luo et al., 2019). It can be applied in different areas that consider "globalization" terms such as employment, economy, politics, etc. Especially the effect of globalization on jobs in developed and developing countries has always been controversial due to its effects on employment. The push for localism can be recognized by many, but not all are ready to practice it locally as it opposes globalization idea.

Localization is about reclaiming "community" from the forces of automation, outsourcing, global trade, and consumerism (Nandi et al., 2021:10-22). As global trade intensifies, corporations are designing strategies to bypass local business laws to circumvent taxes that are too onerous or counterproductive. For example, in the past few years, the E.U. has passed rules allowing non-EU companies to use its market free of charge (Evans et al., 2021). This means that U.S. tech companies can now sell products in Europe and then shut down their E.U. businesses and open headquarters in Ireland, where they pay no corporate tax. Many companies that benefit from these free-trade agreements have moved their manufacturing to China and other countries.

Globalization's chief goal is to take power away from local economies and put it in the hands of transnational corporations (Hines, 2013). The policies being pushed by the World Trade Organization (WTO) and international financial institutions such as the World Bank and IMF inhibit local policies and hinder efforts to rebuild local economies through localization.

Globalization activists such as Naomi Klein and Larry Summers advocate pushing globalization from the world's wealthiest countries to the poorest. This could be done through managed globalization in which governments invest more in their local economies. However, critics argue that it will continue to rely on exploitation at the expense of local economies (Klein, 2020). While globalization is viewed as neutral, it has changed society's population growth, which has led to the formation of many people without any employment. This is one reason we are losing our identity.

Global Localization

Global localization is known as the process of tailoring a brand's message or product to the local language, culture, and customs. Another stage in delivering a customized client experience is localization. Localized content must be a significant component of the entire marketing plan for global marketing teams. People today are increasingly conscious of globalization and want to take local actions. So, "Glocalization" is a new term used to explain how the globe is changing. "Globalization" and "localization" are combined to form "glocalization." The phrase refers to a good or service that is created, offered, and sold internationally but also modified to satisfy customers in local markets. In other words, "glocalization" refers to the simultaneous ownership of global and local entities dependent on each other (Rosen, 2021).

Lately, there has been an increasing trend toward using the services offered by small business owners. The growth in popularity of small businesses is due to two main characteristics. First, small businesses have highly personal services as they usually create a personal connection with their customers by providing them with quality products and services. Second, small business owners have fewer overhead costs, allowing them to provide better prices and also providing them with the resources they need to thrive (Hoffin, 2020:27-48). This is especially evident in the case of small online businesses.

The advertisement of local products has become a major feature among consumers in recent years. Local production can greatly increase profits for businesses and local communities (Porter and Kramer, 2019). Local produce is often more affordable than imported products and helps to support local communities.

Glocalization efforts use culturally sensitive media and advertising to promote local audiences' acceptance of foreign goods (Ephraim, 2019). But our goods are not even from another country. Since our product is new to most people, the most important factor in achieving worldwide acceptance is our "local" strategy. We must design goods that appeal to you and fit into your lifestyle and reassure you that we are doing it correctly.

The desire for local products is increasing in both developed and developing countries. There are multiple reasons for the desire for local products. In developed countries, there are health concerns about imported foods and cultural and economic issues such as cheap labor and outsourcing (Hollweg, 2019). Consumers want to know that their money is going back into the community they live in rather than to an international company's corporate headquarters. In developing countries, there are food safety and economic concerns. People need to know that their product is safe to eat and can help them become more economically stable.

Glocalization is very influential in how businesses market their products to local consumers. It has become much more interesting for businesses to understand what local consumers want when they produce their goods than it is to produce goods that appeal to people of other cultures simply. Globalization is becoming a much more common topic in media and businesses. Globalization has been moving rapidly throughout the world for hundreds of years, but globalization awareness is increasing tremendously today (Khan et al., 2020). This increase in the amount and quality of research makes each new discovery much more impactful on global economic affairs.

McDonald's glocalized its products around the world

McDonald's, one of the most frequently cited glocalization instances, has more than 69 million consumers globally. It has perfected tailoring its branding, menu offerings, and dietary needs to each target region (Crane et al., 2019).

Big Macs without cheese are available at kosher McDonald's locations in Israel. For Hindus who don't consume beef, their Indian restaurants mostly provide chicken, lamb, and vegetarian fare. In India, McDonald's sells items like the Veg Maharaja Mac and the Chicken Maharaja Mac (a grilled chicken double patty with habanero sauce) (Singireddy, 2020).

The McArabia Chicken is a pita sandwich with two grilled chicken or beef patties, tomato, onion, lettuce, and garlic sauce available in fast food chain restaurants in Arab nations (Khan and Khan, 2013). In contrast, you may pair your Big Mac with a local beer in several European nations; it should be no surprise that the German McDonald's was the first to offer beer on its menu.

McDonald's understands food's importance to people's cultures and has adapted its brand and offerings appropriately. Consequently, nations worldwide now value their products and are familiar with their brand (Tien, 2019). McDonald's has embraced global branding as well. To establish a more eco-friendly image in Europe, the company switched from its customary red backdrop to a deep hunter-green one (Cowin, 2011).

Global integration is the process through which a business merges several activities globally to run according to the same guidelines (Weber, 2013). This requires businesses to become more efficient and effective. One of the major drivers behind global integration is to reduce costs. When a business can make one product for one market, it can reduce its cost of production (per unit) (Bertram, 2019). This is known as economies of scale. If a business spreads its fixed costs over a larger customer base, it can realize greater profits.

Strengthening local economics through glocalization will likely positively affect global integration. For example, these local markets will need more communication and technology. This will allow for a greater exchange of information, in turn improving global integration (McDonagh and Commins, 2018).

While McDonald's has been widely criticized for its negative impact on local economies and culture, it's undeniably had a huge impact on global integration. With over 36,000 locations in 119 countries, McDonald's has made it easy to find their fries and Big Macs almost anywhere (D'Souza, 2018). The sheer number of locations and standardized menu makes McDonald's one of the most successful glocalization efforts thus far

How to strengthen local economies

Education Programs

Educating locals on the importance of buying local products and their options for locally produced goods is a big step towards building a sustainable local economy (Scheyvens and Laeis, 2022). Children should be taught the importance of taking care of their environment and how harmful it is to the planet to consume imported goods. The government can also help educate its citizens by providing incentives for businesses that produce goods locally.

This will serve as a great incentive for businesses and motivate them to increase their output of locally produced goods.

Local economies, where people live and work, are where economies start. The economy is a component of culture; it is influenced by our actions, values, and aspirations. Inclusive economies aim to lessen residents' inequality by allocating resources to enhance the welfare and foster long-term prosperity (Feldman et al., 2016). For anybody who wants to be a change leader in this field, Coady's certificate programs in Mobilizing Assets for Citizen-Driven Development, Livelihoods & Markets, and Community-Based Financial Inclusion offer an extensive bundle of specific skills and knowledge. Additionally, every credential alone teaches learners the skills and information they need for a specialized job in this subject.

Community-Based Financial Inclusion, for example, is structured for a wide range of professionals interested in launching and operating a financial service business as a microfinance institution (MFI) (Ledgerwood et al., 2013).

Knowledge Nuts offers training on the most relevant topics in management, entrepreneurship, marketing, and small business, including soft and hard skills training. The company's public seminars are led by subject matter experts who conduct hands-on workshops after every topic (Cole, 2010). These workshops help learners apply what they learned in their everyday life.

Some institutes, like the Coady International Institute, offer education programs that are intensely participative classes created to improve the comprehension and productivity of leaders operating in various fields (Boni and Velasco, 2020). The programs employ a wide range of presenting, case study, experiential, and participatory teaching strategies. The workshops provide leaders the chance to share ideas and exchange experiences with international colleagues, gain knowledge from the experience and skills of competent facilitators, and are inspired by global innovations and pertinent action research.

The Coady Institute supports strategies for expanding local economies' inclusiveness. The Institute does this through market tactics that allow local economies to have a larger input into and profit from local production, community-based microfinance and livelihood programs, and educational initiatives that support women's economic independence (Thorpe, Mathie, and Ghore,

2017). The Institute collaborates with regional partners to create, test, and disseminate ideas that can boost regional economies worldwide. These new developments are regularly included in our educational programs' curricula.

When the citizens are educated, this can enhance advance in global integration. Educated individuals often make the decisions and policies that affect economic globalization and international agreements. People may prosper in the economy's globalization and lessen its negative effects with the help of education, which equips them with the skills and values they need.

REFERENCES ON GLOBALIZATION

'Sinha, S., 2018. Gender digital divide in India: Impacting women's participation in the labour market. In Reflecting on India's development (pp. 293-310). Springer, Singapore.

Altieri, M.A. and Nicholls, C.I., 2020. Agro ecology and the reconstruction of a post-COVID-19 agriculture. The Journal of Peasant Studies, 47(5), pp.881-898.

Arndt, C., Halikiopoulou, D. and Vrakopoulos, C., 2022. The centre-periphery divide and attitudes towards climate change measures among Western Europeans. Environmental Politics, pp.1-26.

Aurambout, J.P., Gkoumas, K. and Ciuffo, B., 2019. Last mile delivery by drones: An estimation of viable market potential and access to citizens across European cities. European Transport Research Review, 11(1), pp.1-21.

Bailey, N., 2012. The role, organisation and contribution of community enterprise to urban regeneration policy in the U.K. Progress in planning, 77(1), pp.1-35.

Bertram, N., Fuchs, S., Mischke, J., Palter, R., Strube, G. and Woetzel, J., 2019. Modular construction: From projects to products. McKinsey & Company: Capital Projects & Infrastructure, pp.1-34.

Boni, A. and Velasco, D., 2020. Epistemic capabilities and epistemic injustice: What is the role of higher education in fostering epistemic contributions of marginalized knowledge producers? Global Justice: Theory Practice Rhetoric, 12(01), pp.1-26.

Bradford, A., 2020. The Brussels effect: How the European Union rules the world. Oxford University Press, USA.

Bryson, J.R. and Vanchan, V., 2020. COVID-19 and alternative conceptualisations of value and risk in GPN research. Tijdschrift voor economische en sociale geografie, 111(3), pp.530-542.

Casaglia, A., Coletti, R., Lizotte, C., Agnew, J., Mamadouh, V. and Minca, C., 2020. Interventions on European nationalist populism and bordering in time of emergencies. Political Geography, 82, p.102238.

CHACKO, P., 2021. A new quest for self-reliance: East Asia and Indian economic nationalism. The Journal of Indian and Asian Studies, 2(02), p.2140005.

Cole, M.L., 2010. Leadership development for independent school leaders: A model. Texas Christian University.

Cowin, E., 2011. The evolution of U.S. corporate logos a semiotic analysis.

Crane, A., Matten, D., Glozer, S. and Spence, L., 2019. Business ethics: Managing corporate citizenship and sustainability in the age of globalization. Oxford University Press, USA.

D'Souza, V., 2018. "Unethical advertising through social media"- A case study investigating ethical marketing issues in the fast food industry of Ireland (Doctoral dissertation, Dublin Business School).

Ephraim, P.E., 2019. Louvre Abu Dhabi: Social media in marketing culture. In Proceedings of the 5th World Conference on Media and Mass Communication (Vol. 5, No. 1, pp. 49-57).

Espa, I. and Marín Durán, G., 2018. Renewable energy subsidies and WTO Law: Time to rethink the case for reform beyond Canada–Renewable Energy/FIT Program. Journal of international economic law, 21(3), pp.621-653.

Evans, S., Mehling, M.A., Ritz, R.A. and Sammon, P., 2021. Border carbon adjustments and industrial competitiveness in a European Green Deal. Climate Policy, 21(3), pp.307-317.

Feder-Madoff, M.A., 2022. Introducing Things. Performing Craft in Mexico: Artisans, Aesthetics, and the Power of Translation, p.1.

Feldman, M., Hadjimichael, T., Lanahan, L. and Kemeny, T., 2016. The logic of economic development: A definition and model for investment. Environment and Planning C: Government and Policy, 34(1), pp.5-21.

Helyer, R. and Lee, D., 2014. The role of work experience in the future employability of higher education graduates. Higher Education Quarterly, 68(3), pp.348-372.

Hines, C., 2013. Localization: A global manifesto. Routledge.

Hoffman, K., 2020. Glocalization, bricolage and black metal: Towards a music-centric youth culture simultaneously exemplifying the global and the glocal. Metal Music Studies, 6(1), pp.27-48.

Hollweg, C.H., 2019. Global value chains and employment in developing economies. Global Value Chain Development Report 2019, p.63.

James, P., 2014. Urban sustainability in theory and practice: circles of sustainability. Routledge.

Khan, M. and Khan, M.M., 2013. I'm lovin' it"—Around the World: A Case Study of McDonald's "Glocalization. In SAGE Business Cases. International CHRIE.

Khan, N., Hassan, A.U., Fahad, S. and Naushad, M., 2020. Factors affecting the tourism industry and its impacts on the global economy of the world. Available at SSRN 3559353.

Klein, N., 2020. On fire: The (burning) case for a green new deal. Simon & Schuster.Klein, N., 2020. On fire: The (burning) case for a green new deal. Simon & Schuster.

Ledgerwood, J., Earne, J. and Nelson, C. eds., 2013. The new microfinance handbook: A financial market system perspective. World Bank Publications.

Luo, Y., Zhang, H. and Bu, J., 2019. Developed country MNEs investing in developing economies: Progress and prospect. Journal of International Business Studies, 50(4), pp.633-667.

McDonagh, P. and Commins, P., 2018. Globalization and Rural Development: Demographic Revitalization, Entrepreneurs and Small Business Formation in the West of Ireland. In Local Responses to Global Integration (pp. 179-202). Routledge.

McGenity, T.J., Gessesse, A., Hallsworth, J.E., Garcia Cela, E., Verheecke-Vaessen, C., Wang, F., Chavarría, M., Haggblom, M.M., Molin, S., Danchin, A. and Smid, E.J., 2020. Visualizing the invisible: class excursions to ignite children's enthusiasm for microbes. Microbial Biotechnology, 13(4), pp.844-887.

Morschheuser, B., Hamari, J. and Maedche, A., 2019. Cooperation or competition–When do people contribute more? A field experiment on gamification of crowdsourcing. International Journal of Human-Computer Studies, 127, pp.7-24.

Nandi, S., Sarkis, J., Hervani, A.A. and Helms, M.M., 2021. Redesigning supply chains using blockchain-enabled circular economy and COVID-19 experiences. Sustainable Production and Consumption, 27, pp.10-22.

Poppi, F., 2016. Balancing local identity and global audiences: Localized and globalized instances of EIL in corporate websites.

Porter, M.E. and Kramer, M.R., 2019. Creating shared value. In managing sustainable business (pp. 323-346). Springer, Dordrecht.

Porter, M.E. and Kramer, M.R., 2019. Creating shared value. In managing sustainable business (pp. 323-346). Springer, Dordrecht.

Quayson, M., Bai, C. and Osei, V., 2020. Digital inclusion for resilient post-COVID-19 supply chains: Smallholder farmer perspectives. IEEE Engineering Management Review, 48(3), pp.104-110.

Rodríguez-Pose, A. and Storper, M., 2020. Housing, urban growth and inequalities: The limits to deregulation and upzoning in reducing economic and spatial inequality. Urban Studies, 57(2), pp.223-248.

Rodríguez-Pose, A. and Storper, M., 2020. Housing, urban growth and inequalities: The limits to deregulation and upzoning in reducing economic and spatial inequality. Urban Studies, 57(2), pp.223-248.

Rosen, R., 2021. The glocalization of the shared society concept in Israel. Conflict Resolution Quarterly, 39(2), pp.161-177.

Sabaratnam, M., 2020. Is I.R. theory white? Racialised subject-positioning in three canonical texts. Millennium, 49(1), pp.3-31.

Sahan, E., 2019. Greed does not have to drive business: the role of Fair Trade Enterprises as proof of concept. Journal of Fair Trade, 1(2), pp.14-23.

Sasaki, I., Ravasi, D. and Micelotta, E., 2019. Family firms as institutions: Cultural reproduction and status maintenance among multi-centenary shinise in Kyoto. Organization Studies, 40(6), pp.793-831.

Scheyvens, R. and Laeis, G., 2022. Linkages between tourist resorts, local food production and the sustainable development goals. In Recentering Tourism Geographies in the 'Asian Century' (pp. 139-161). Routledge.

Sharova, L. and Cassany, D., 2019. Bronies learning English in the digital wild. Language Learning & Technology. 2019 Feb; 23 (1): 127-44.

Singireddy, M., 2020. Mcdonald's: Global Marketing. International Journal of Health and Economic Development, 6(2), pp.16-27.

Soper, K., 2020. Post-growth living: For an alternative hedonism. Verso Books.

Thorpe, J., Mathie, A. and Ghore, Y., 2017. A typology of market-based approaches to include the most marginalised.

Tien, N.H., 2019. Customization and Standardization of the Business Strategy of Foreign Enterprises in Vietnam–the McDonald's Case and the Fast Food Sector.". International journal of research in marketing management and sales, 1(2), pp.44-50.

Weber, Y., 2013. A comprehensive guide to mergers & acquisitions: Managing the critical success factors across every stage of the M&A process. F.T. Press.

Zhu, J.S., 2019. Chinese multinationals' approach to international human resource management: A longitudinal study. The International Journal of Human Resource Management, 30(14), pp.2166-2185.

Roy, D., Tripathy, S., Kar, S.K., Sharma, N., Verma, S.K. and Kaushal, V., 2020. Study of knowledge, attitude, anxiety & perceived mental healthcare need in Indian population during COVID-19 pandemic. Asian journal of psychiatry, 51, p.102083.

Kumar, S., Maheshwari, V., Prabhu, J., Prasanna, M., Jayalakshmi, P., Suganya, P., Malar, B.A. and Jothikumar, R., 2020. Social economic impact of COVID-19 outbreak in India. International Journal of Pervasive Computing and Communications.

Hopewell, K., 2015. Different paths to power: The rise of Brazil, India and China at the World Trade Organization. Review of international political economy, 22(2), pp.311-338.

Cooke, F.L., Saini, D.S. and Wang, J., 2014. Talent management in China and India: A comparison of management perceptions and human resource practices. Journal of World Business, 49(2), pp.225-235.

Randhir, T. (2016). Globalization impacts on local commons: multiscale strategies for socioeconomic and ecological resilience. International Journal of the Commons, 10(1).

Bardhan, A. D., Jaffee, D. M., & Kroll, C. A. (2004). Foreign Outsourcing and Domestic Industry. Globalization and a High-Tech Economy: California, the United States and Beyond, 91-114.

Xiaoman, W., Majeed, A., Vasbieva, D. G., Yameogo, C. E. W., & Hussain, N. (2021). Natural resources abundance, economic globalization, and carbon emissions: Advancing sustainable development agenda. Sustainable development, 29(5), 1037-1048.

Rembet, E. C. S., Saerang, D. P. E., & Rumokoy, F. (2014). The Effects of Globalization on Local Company in Manado: a Case Study of CV. Central Bukit Moria Manado. Jurnal EMBA: Jurnal Riset Ekonomi, Manajemen, Bisnis dan Akuntansi, 2(2).

Rodrik, D. (2018). Populism and the economics of globalization. Journal of international business policy, 1(1), 12-33.

Thompson, L. J., & Wadley, D. A. (2018). Countering globalisation and managerialism: Relationist ethics in social work. International Social Work, 61(5), 706-723.

Bretos, I., & Marcuello, C. (2017). Revisiting globalization challenges and opportunities in the development of cooperatives. Annals of Public and Cooperative Economics, 88(1), 47-73.

Lin, J. Y., & Wang, X. (2018). Trump economics and China–US trade imbalances. Journal of Policy Modeling, 40(3), 579-600.

Merga, B., & Haji, J. (2019). Economic importance of chickpea: Production, value, and world trade. Cogent Food & Agriculture, 5(1), 1615718.

Hopewell, K. (2015). Different paths to power: The rise of Brazil, India and China at the World Trade Organization. Review of international political economy, 22(2), 311-338.

Rababah, A., Al-Haddad, L., Sial, M.S., Chunmei, Z. and Cherian, J., 2020. Analyzing the effects of COVID-19 pandemic on the financial performance of Chinese listed companies. Journal of Public Affairs, 20(4), p.e2440.

Gilli, A., & Gilli, M. (2018). Why China has not caught up yet: military-technological superiority and the limits of imitation, reverse engineering, and cyber espionage. International Security, 43(3), 141-189.

Law, W. W. (2014). Understanding China's curriculum reform for the 21st century. Journal of Curriculum Studies, 46(3), 332-360.

Brooks, S. G., & Wohlforth, W. C. (2015). The rise and fall of the great powers in the twenty-first century: China's rise and the fate of America's global position. International security, 40(3), 7-53.

Liu, W., Dunford, M., & Gao, B. (2018). A discursive construction of the Belt and Road Initiative: From neo-liberal to inclusive globalization. Journal of Geographical Sciences, 28(9), 1199-1214.

Brødsgaard, K. E. (2014). Globalization and public sector reform in China. In Globalization and public sector reform in China (pp. 19-40). Routledge.

Xu, J., & Xia, Z. (2019). Traditional Chinese medicine (TCM)–Does its contemporary business booming and globalization really reconfirm its medical efficacy & safety?. Medicine in Drug Discovery, 1, 100003.

Wang, X. S. (2015). The Chinese Economy in Crisis: State Capacity and Tax Reform: State Capacity and Tax Reform. Routledge.

Lin, J. Y. (2017). The rise of China and its implications for economics and other developing countries. Area Development and Policy, 2(2), 109-119.

Zheng, S., Kahn, M.E., Sun, W. and Luo, D., 2014. Incentives for China's urban mayors to mitigate pollution externalities: The role of the central government and public environmentalism. Regional Science and Urban Economics, 47, pp.61-71.

Tan, Y. (2014). Transparency without democracy: The unexpected effects of C hina's environmental disclosure policy. Governance, 27(1), 37-62.

Zeng, D. Z. (2015). Global experiences with special economic zones: Focus on China and Africa. World Bank Policy Research Working Paper, (7240).

Zheng, W., Singh, K. and Mitchell, W., 2015. Buffering and enabling: The impact of interlocking political ties on firm survival and sales growth. Strategic Management Journal, 36(11), pp.1615-1636.

Xie, Y., Zhang, C. and Lai, Q., 2014. China's rise as a major contributor to science and technology. Proceedings of the National Academy of Sciences, 111(26), pp.9437-9442.

Chatterji, S., Byles, J., Cutler, D., Seeman, T. and Verdes, E., 2015. Health, functioning, and disability in older adults—present status and future implications. The lancet, 385(9967), pp.563-575.

Wang, X. S. (2015). The Chinese Economy in Crisis: State Capacity and Tax Reform: State Capacity and Tax Reform. Routledge.

Hopewell, K., 2015. Different paths to power: The rise of Brazil, India and China at the World Trade Organization. Review of international political economy, 22(2), pp.311-338.

Willis, G., Genchev, S.E. and Chen, H., 2016. Supply chain learning, integration, and flexibility performance: an empirical study in India. The International Journal of Logistics Management.

Malik, M.R. and Prasad, R., 2015. Indian carpet industry after trade liberalization. Problems and prospects. Academic Journal of Economic Studies, 1(3), pp.79-88.

Tien, N.H., Phu, P.P. and Chi, D.T.P., 2019. The role of international marketing in international business strategy. International journal of research in marketing management and sales, 1(2), pp.134-138.

Bagli, S. and Adhikary, M., 2014. FDI inflow and economic growth in India an empirical analysis. Economic Affairs, 59(1), p.23.

Raichurkar, P. and Ramachandran, M., 2015. Recent trends and developments in textile industry in India. International Journal on Textile Engineering & Processes, 1(4), pp.47-50.

Siddiqui, K., 2016. Will the growth of the BRICs cause a shift in the global balance of economic power in the 21st century?. International Journal of Political Economy, 45(4), pp.315-338.

Nolan, P., 2014. Chinese firms, global firms: industrial policy in the age of globalization. Routledge.

Lacal-Arántegui, R., 2019. Globalization in the wind energy industry: contribution and economic impact of European companies. Renewable Energy, 134, pp.612-628.

Lechner, F.J. and Boli, J. eds., 2020. The globalization reader. John Wiley & Sons.

Stearns, P.N., 2020. The industrial revolution in world history. Routledge.

.Korotayev, A.V. and LePoire, D.J., 2020. The 21st Century Singularity and Global Futures. Springer International Publishing.

Korotayev, A.V. and LePoire, D.J., 2020. The 21st Century Singularity and Global Futures. Springer International Publishing.

Pradhan, R., 2015. India's Soft Power in Central Asia: Why it must Act on the Look North Policy. Mainstream Weekly.

Ake, C., 2019. The new world order: a view from Africa. In Whose World Order? (pp. 19-42). Routledge.

Alexander, R., 2020. Emerging roles of lead buyer governance for sustainability across global production networks. Journal of Business Ethics, 162(2), pp.269-290.

Autio, E., Mudambi, R. and Yoo, Y., 2021. Digitalization and globalization in a turbulent world: Centrifugal and centripetal forces. Global Strategy Journal, 11(1), pp.3-16.

Bianchi, R.V. and de Man, F., 2021. Tourism, inclusive growth and decent work: A political economy critique. Journal of Sustainable Tourism, 29(2-3), pp.353-371.

Carroll, T., Gonzalez-Vicente, R. and Jarvis, D.S., 2019. Capital, conflict and convergence: A political understanding of neoliberalism and its relationship to capitalist transformation. Globalizations, 16(6), pp.778-803.

Chow, D.C., 2020. US Trade Infallibility and the Crisis of the World Trade Organization. Mich. St. L. Rev., p.599.

Contractor, F., Foss, N.J., Kundu, S. and Lahiri, S., 2019. Viewing global strategy through a microfoundations lens. Global Strategy Journal, 9(1), pp.3-18.

Gaspar, V., Amaglobeli, M.D., Garcia-Escribano, M.M., Prady, D. and Soto, M., 2019. Fiscal policy and development: Human, social, and physical investments for the SDGs. International Monetary Fund.

Gaughan, P.H. and Javalgi, R.R.G., 2018. A framework for analyzing international business and legal ethical standards. Business Horizons, 61(6), pp.813-822.

Hancock, J.F., 2021. Spices, Scents and Silk: Catalysts of World Trade. CABI.

He, Q., Wang, N., Yang, Z., He, Z. and Jiang, B., 2019. Competitive collection under channel inconvenience in closed-loop supply chain. European Journal of Operational Research, 275(1), pp.155-166.

Kato, M., Saito, N., Matsushita, R., Ueno, M., Izawa, S., Maruyama, Y., Sugita, H., Ono, F., Muroi, R., Miyazaki, Y. and Yamana, J., 2022. Philosophy of education in a new key: Voices from Japan. Educational Philosophy and Theory, 54(8), pp.1113-1129.

Klein, M.C. and Pettis, M., 2020. Trade wars are class wars: How rising inequality distorts the global economy and threatens international peace. Yale University Press.

Konadu-Agyemang, K. and Takyi, B.K., 2018. Structural adjustment programs and the political economy of development and underdevelopment in Ghana. In IMF and World Bank Sponsored Structural Adjustment Programs in Africa (pp. 17-40). Routledge.

Mehedintu, A., Soava, G. and Sterpu, M., 2019. Remittances, migration and gross domestic product from Romania's perspective. Sustainability, 12(1), p.212.

O'Rourke, K.H., 2019. Economic history and contemporary challenges to Globalization. The Journal of Economic History, 79(2), pp.356-382.

Ershov, B.A., Perevozchikova, L.S. and Romanova, E.V., 2019. Globalization and intensification of spiritual values in Russia in the philosophical aspect. In 6th International Conference on

Education and Social Sciences Abstracts & Proceedings (pp. 208-212).

Burlacu, S., Gutu, C. and Matei, F.O., 2018. Globalization–pros and cons. Calitatea, 19(S1), pp.122-125.

Oi, S., Fukuda, M. and Sako, S., 2020. The Japanese journalist in transition: Continuity and change. The Global Journalist in the 21st Century (pp. 52-65). Routledge.

Ahmed, Z., Ahmad, M., Rjoub, H., Kalugina, O.A. and Hussain, N., 2021. Economic growth, renewable energy consumption, and ecological footprint: Exploring the role of environmental regulations and democracy in sustainable development. Sustainable Development.

Alam, G.M., Forhad, A.R. and Ismail, I.A., 2020. Can education as an 'International Commodity'be the backbone or cane of a nation in the era of fourth industrial revolution?-A Comparative study. Technological Forecasting and Social Change, 159, p.120184.

Alvarado, F., 2018. World inequality report 2018. In World Inequality Report 2018. Harvard University Press.

Antràs, P., 2020. De-globalisation? Global value chains in the post-COVID-19 age (No. w28115). National Bureau of Economic Research.

Ayeb, H. and Bush, R., 2019. Food Insecurity and Revolution in the Middle East and North Africa: Agrarian Questions in Egypt and Tunisia. Anthem press.

Bianchi, F. and Civelli, A., 2015. Globalization and inflation: Evidence from a time-varying VAR. Review of Economic Dynamics, 18(2), pp.406-433.

Brandolini, A., Gambacorta, R. and Rosolia, A., 2018. Inequality amid income stagnation: Italy over the last quarter of a century. Bank of Italy Occasional Paper, (442).

Carlson, M.J., Wimer, C. and Haskins, R., 2022. Changing Work, Changing Families, and Public Policies toward Low-Income Families. RSF: The Russell Sage Foundation Journal of the Social Sciences, 8(5), pp.1-22.

Charles, K.K., Hurst, E. and Schwartz, M., 2019. The transformation of manufacturing and the decline in U.S. employment. NBER Macroeconomics Annual, 33(1), pp.307-372.

Chen, H. and Siklos, P.L., 2020. Oceans Apart? China and Other Systemically Important Economies. China and Other Systemically Important Economies (March 11, 2020).

Cooke, S.J., Twardek, W.M., Lynch, A.J., Cowx, I.G., Olden, J.D., Funge-Smith, S., Lorenzen, K., Arlinghaus, R., Chen, Y., Weyl, O.L. and Nyboer, E.A., 2021. A global perspective on the influence of the COVID-19 pandemic on freshwater fish biodiversity. Biological Conservation, 253, p.108932.

Da SILVA, P.E.R.E.R.I.R.A. and LA–MOJON, B., 2019. Exiting low inflation traps by "consensus": nominal wages and price stability. Based on the Keynote Speech at the Eighth High-level Policy Dialogue between the Eurosystem and Latin American Central Banks, Cartagena de Indias, Colombia, pp.28-29.

Daphne, P., 2019. The global justice movement in Europe. In Routledge Handbook of Contemporary European Social Movements (pp. 142-154). Routledge.

de Soyres, F., Santacreu, A.M. and Young, H.L., 2022. Demand-Supply imbalance during the Covid-19 pandemic: the role of fiscal policy. International Finance Discussion Paper, (1353).

Elhefnawy, N., 2020. Keynesian Fordism and Neoliberal Financialization: A Comparison of Economic Models. Available at SSRN 3685990.

Erixon, F., 2018. The economic benefits of globalization for business and consumers. European Centre for International Political Economy.

Faria-e-Castro, M., 2021. Fiscal policy during a pandemic. Journal of Economic Dynamics and Control, 125, p.104088.

Flaherty, T.M. and Rogowski, R., 2021. Rising inequality as a threat to the liberal international order. International Organization, 75(2), pp.495-523.

Fukuyama, F., 2018. Against identity politics: the new tribalism and the crisis of democracy. Foreign Aff., 97, p.90.

Gavin, W.T., 2018. Monetary policy regimes and the real interest rate. Available at SSRN 3194985.

Groenewegen, A., Rutten, F.H., Mosterd, A. and Hoes, A.W., 2020. Epidemiology of heart failure. European journal of heart failure, 22(8), pp.1342-1356.

Guerrieri, V., Lorenzoni, G., Straub, L. and Werning, I., 2021. Monetary policy in times of structural reallocation. University of Chicago, Becker Friedman Institute for Economics Working Paper, (2021-111).

Ha, J., Kose, M.A. and Ohnsorge, F., 2021. One-stop source: A global database of inflation.

Harding, S., 2019. State of the field: Latin American decolonial philosophies of science. Studies in History and Philosophy of Science Part A, 78, pp.48-63.

Hazell, J., Herrero, J., Nakamura, E. and Steinsson, J., 2022. The slope of the Phillips Curve: evidence from U.S. states. The Quarterly Journal of Economics, 137(3), pp.1299-1344.

Helmboldt, N.E., West, T. and Hardy, B.H., 2021. African Economic Policy. Strategies for African Development, p.331.

Henckens, T., 2021. Scarce mineral resources: Extraction, consumption and limits of sustainability. Resources, Conservation and Recycling, 169, p.105511.

Hopper, T., Lassou, P. and Soobaroyen, T., 2017. Globalisation, accounting and developing countries. Critical Perspectives on Accounting, 43, pp.125-148.

Kamin, S.B., 2011. Financial globalization and monetary policy.

Kelly, J., 2018. Social democracy and anti-communism: Allan Flanders and British industrial relations in the early post-war period. In British Trade Unions and Industrial Politics (pp. 208-237). Routledge.

Koddenbrock, K., Kvangraven, I.H. and Sylla, N.S., 2020. Beyond financialisation: The need for a longue durée understanding of finance in imperialism.

Koester, G., Lis, E., Nickel, C., Osbat, C. and Smets, F., 2021. Understanding low inflation in the euro area from 2013 to 2019: cyclical and structural drivers. ECB Occasional Paper, (2021280).

Kwan, C.H., 2020. The China-US trade war: Deep-rooted causes, shifting focus and uncertain prospects. Asian Economic Policy Review, 15(1), pp.55-72.

Labonté, R., 2019. Trade, investment and public health: compiling the evidence, assembling the arguments. Globalization and health, 15(1), pp.1-12.

Latos, S., 2018. Real Wage Effects of Japan's Monetary Policy. ORDO, 2018(69), pp.177-215.

Lodge, D., Everett, M., Bandt, O.D., Georgiadis, G., Ca'Zorzi, M., Lastauskas, P., Carluccio, J., Parrága, S., Cova, P., Attinasi, M.G. and Mozzanica, M.B., 2021. The implications of globalisation for the ECB monetary policy strategy.

Lourenco, L., Silveira, D., Oliveira, G. and Vasconcelos, C., 2021. Do Antidumping Measures Increase Market Power? Evidence From Latin American Countries. The International Trade Journal, pp.1-27.

Mancini-Griffoli, T., Peria, M.S.M., Agur, I., Ari, A., Kiff, J., Popescu, A. and Rochon, C., 2018. Casting light on central bank digital currency. IMF staff discussion note, 8(18), pp.1-39.

Manduca, R.A., 2019. The contribution of national income inequality to regional economic divergence. Social Forces, 98(2), pp.622-648.

McMillan, M., Rodrik, D. and Verduzco-Gallo, Í., 2014. Globalization, structural change, and productivity growth, with an update on Africa. World Development, 63, pp.11-32.

Mogaji, E. and Nguyen, N.P., 2021. Transportation satisfaction of disabled passengers: Evidence from a developing country. Transportation research part D: transport and environment, 98, p.102982.

Morgan, S., Pfaff, A. and Wolfersberger, J., 2022. Environmental Policies Benefit Economic Development: Implications of Economic Geography. Annual Review of Resource Economics, 14.

Ray, P. and Pal, P., 2022. Festival of Death: Global Stock Markets during the Pandemic. In The Impact of COVID-19 on India and the Global Order (pp. 189-210). Springer, Singapore.

Rodríguez-Pose, A., 2020. Institutions and the fortunes of territories. Regional Science Policy & Practice, 12(3), pp.371-386.

Russell-Wood, A.J.R., 2020. Colonial Brazil: the gold cycle, c. 1690–1750. In Mines of Silver and Gold in the Americas (pp. 321-383). Routledge.

Saavedra-Rivano, N., 2021. Chile and Regional Integration. In Cooperation or Rivalry? (pp. 97-111). Routledge.

Smith, M., Zidar, O.M. and Zwick, E., 2021. Top wealth in America: New estimates and implications for taxing the rich (No. w29374). National Bureau of Economic Research.

Stevenson, B., 2020. The initial impact of COVID-19 on labor market outcomes across groups and the potential for permanent scarring. The Hamilton Project.

Stiglitz, J., 2016. Globalization and its new discontents. Project Syndicate, 5(8), pp.2-3.

Sur, M., 2021. Jungle passports: Fences, mobility, and citizenship at the Northeast India-Bangladesh border. University of Pennsylvania Press.

Therborn, G., 2020. Sweden's turn to economic inequality, 1982–2019. Structural Change and Economic Dynamics, 52, pp.159-166.

Volz, U., Beirne, J., Ambrosio Preudhomme, N., Fenton, A., Mazzacurati, E., Renzhi, N. and Stampe, J., 2020. Climate change and sovereign risk.

Yavorsky, J.E., Keister, L.A., Qian, Y. and Nau, M., 2019. Women in the one percent: Gender dynamics in top income positions. American Sociological Review, 84(1), pp.54-81.

Zhang, R., Zhang, H., Gao, W., Li, T. and Yang, S., 2022. The Dynamic Effects of Oil Price Shocks on Exchange Rates—From a Time-Varying Perspective. Sustainability, 14(14), p.8452.

Pegan, G., Vianelli, D. and de Luca, P., 2020. Strategic Entry Modes and Country of Origin Effect. In International Marketing Strategy (pp. 25-38). Springer, Cham.

Peters, M.A., 2021. The ancient Silk Road and the birth of merchant capitalism. Educational Philosophy and Theory, 53(10), pp.955-961.

Roberts, L.L., 2019. Changing worldwide attitudes toward homosexuality: The influence of global and region-specific cultures, 1981–2012. Social science research, 80, pp.114-131.

SIDDIQUI, K., 2020. The Political Economy of the Slave Trade, Capital Accumulation and the Rise of Britain. World.

Thompson, M.N. and Dahling, J.J., 2019. Employment and poverty: Why work matters in understanding poverty. American Psychologist, 74(6), p.673.

Tight, M., 2021. Globalization and internationalization as frameworks for higher education research. Research Papers in Education, 36(1), pp.52-74.

Van Barneveld, K., Quinlan, M., Kriesler, P., Junor, A., Baum, F., Chowdhury, A., Junankar, P.N., Clibborn, S., Flanagan, F., Wright, C.F. and Friel, S., 2020. The COVID-19 pandemic: Lessons on building more equal and sustainable societies. The economic and labour relations review, 31(2), pp.133-157.

Wang, Z. and Sun, Z., 2021. From Globalization to regionalization: The United States, China, and the post-Covid-19 world economic order. Journal of Chinese Political Science, 26(1), pp.69-87.

Yaya, S., Otu, A. and Labonté, R., 2020. Globalisation in the time of COVID-19: repositioning Africa to meet the immediate and remote challenges. Globalization and Health, 16(1), pp.1-7.

Young, B., 2018. Financialization, unconventional monetary policy and gender inequality. In Handbook on the international political economy of gender (pp. 241-251). Edward Elgar Publishing.

Made in the USA
Monee, IL
11 November 2026

a47aa993-5f12-41ef-8f5d-592da11e25b6R01